MW01673683

Dance with Samsara

Dance with Samsara

Deconstructing Ego's Drama

Cecil Messer

Dance with Samsara
Deconstructing Ego's Drama

Copyright 2022 Cecil Messer

All rights reserved. Permission is granted to copy and use material in this book in the manner consistent with its intended purpose of spiritual awakening and with the provision that the source is credited. Email: cecilmesser7@gmail.com

Publisher's Cataloging-in-Publication Data

Names: Messer, Cecil, author.
Title:, Dance with Samsara, Deconstructing Ego's Drama / Cecil Messer
Revised previous version: Pathways to Enlightenment, a Journey of Discovery and Radical Transformation / Cecil Messer.
Description: Includes bibliographical references. | Asheville, NC: TwoCrows Publishing, 2022.
Identifiers: LCCN: 2022919121 | ISBN: 978-1-7346126-5-3 (Hardcover) | 978-1-7346126-4-6 (pbk.) | 978-1-7346126-6-0 (KDP eBook) | 978-1-7346126-7-7 (Smashwords eBook)
Subjects: LCSH Spirituality. | Spiritual life. | Enlightenment (Buddhism) | Meditation. | Self-actualization (Psychology) | Happiness. | Mind and body. | BISAC BODY, MIND & SPIRIT / Meditation. | RELIGION / Buddhism (PHILOSOPHY). | SELF-HELP / Spiritual.
Classification: LCC BQ5612 .M485 2020 | DDC 294.3/444--dc23

TwoCrows Publishing
Asheville, NC, USA

Dedication

To each precious teacher,
human or otherwise,
who appeared in the guise of
friend or enemy
and briefly touched my heart.

Illustrations

Contents

PART TWO: THE APPROACH

PART THREE: INTEGRATION

Sharing Beauty

Prelude

Sitting in the shade of an umbrella tree
—dying (as are you),
Oblivious to the resonance of death's distant drumming,
The immense sky, profound and unfathomable,
unmoved by its contents,
Deepened its spectral transition in blue
from azure to indigo.

Its spaciousness accommodated the sun's radiance,
who displayed shadows across the mountain ridges.
Softly compliant, sunbeams caressed the warm earth,
enjoying the texture of every pristine peak and valley,

.

Feathery winds frolicked amidst the hedgerows.
Moving freely, they affectionately
combed and waved undulating fields of grain

Occasionally, small clouds passed over,
forming a complementary panorama of
light and shadow on the distant mountains.

As the sun was still bright, the ground beneath the trees
captured ever-changing shadows of leaves
dancing with the breeze.
The portent of nature's imminently coming
period of stillness yet to reveal itself.

(Strangely, amidst the magic of this phantasmagoria,
subtle residues of anxiety tingled my solar plexus -

perhaps a harbinger of uncertainty in the unfolding
beauty of the stillness of heart and mind.)

In the distant background,
Children sounded their delights and displeasures;
In their separate yet parallel society,
Birds too voiced their joys and sorrows.
In resonance with far away traffic noises,
Ground squirrels expressed excitement and fear,
alarming their kin of real or imagined danger.

As one, all elements formed a coherent and rhythmically
changing spectrum of light and sound.
Joy permeated the entire mandala;
Nothing was out of place;
Distractions were not of this time.

Radiant Darkness approached and hovered over her brood,
gently drawing a blanket, enveloping all in love.
Visual patterns faded and sounds returned to their source.
Stillness settled naturally, without coercion,
Compelled not by withdrawal through fear or weariness
but from the spontaneous movement of order and grace.

Once again, wholeness rested in the benediction of
Absolute Luminosity,
The appearance of a new universe signaled and assured by
the dawning of the morning light.

PART ONE

THE GROUND

Chapter One

Introduction

Truth is not a spectrum of colors, but a single coherent beam of light that pierces the heart of delusion and can only be known through the lens of insight—an open mind. The color of truth is stainless and pristine, like the clear light of deep space. Ultimate truth stands alone and knows things as they are in reality

On the other hand, conventional truth only knows the appearance of things. Under the right conditions, we may see a rainbow in the distance; but it disappears if we try to approach it. When we look in a mirror, we see our face and identify with the image. Our face seems to be there but it is not really there. In both cases, the object is there but it is not there. Relative truth is like a spectrum of diverse colors that takes on the hue of the perceiver From a cat's perspective, water is something to drink; from a fish's view, water is a place to live. From some people's perspective, a certain politician is a savior; from another's view, that same politician is a devil in disguise. To approach the real truth, we must first attend to the relative truth of who we are and our current life predicament.

We are unwitting participants, spinning out of control, in samsara—a dualistic world obsessed with: pleasure/pain, gain/loss, fame/insignificance, and praise/blame. Our deluded life experience is marked by the ebb and flow of uncertainty and discontent.

Nevertheless, our actions reflect the belief that our pursuit of self-centered concerns will bring us happiness. Beneath the façade of this delusion, we are vaguely aware of much suffering outside the boundary of our little sphere of being?

For those who wish to confront the causes and conditions of discontent in the present life, there is a journey of inquiry that probes into the very heart of our situation-in-common. It is not a journey of conquest but a path of cooperation with natural laws wherein we may learn to playfully dance with samsara. It is a process of deconstructing ego's drama, the basic cause of our underlying dissatisfaction.

At the most fundamental level, all beings wish to be happy and free of suffering. Nevertheless, we experience delusion and its associated substratum of feelings that arise when conditions are ripe. Positive feelings range from simple pleasures to rapture. Negative feelings range from mild discontent to extreme pain. So-called neutral feelings are marked with uncertainty and the ghost of anxiety. As we may learn from the vistas that open on this path, it becomes evident that all emotions are painful in essence. This inquiry seeks to illuminate the way out of the darkness of uncertainty and confusion into the bright space of joy and peace. It looks into the nature of our mind itself and develops experiential practices that ignite the flame of insight, the insight that knows what is real versus unreal. Its flame burns away false notions just as the sun dissipates the morning mist. Not for the faint of heart, this journey cuts through the painful landscape of ego's obstacles and crosses over the river of no return. Skillful means are given to quicken the unfolding of our innate powers and initiate a process of holistic healing. This inquiry begins by focusing on prerequisite qualities that prepare us to face the reality of our predicament—the fact that most beings experience pervasive discontent and suffering.

Brief meditation practice sessions prepare the soil of the mind and heart to receive the seeds of transformation and connect with a renewing spiritual experience. These meditation practices help us relax into an inwardly oriented state of awareness that goes beyond conceptual understanding. Progressing in stages, each session is an integration that produces a measure of wholeness.

Our Current Predicament

On the surface, we may appear like the smiling face of a donkey with lips drawn back, carefully munching blackberries through a thicket of thorns. We may feel moderately content but others may not: witness the pervasive homelessness, addiction, and poverty in the world. How palatable is the quality of our personal happiness when confronted with the fact of the suffering of others?

We may mask our fundamental dissatisfaction, the feeling that something is not quite right or complete, by fabricating distractions to avoid facing the issue. Nevertheless, these realities inform our subconscious mind and mark our every action.

Can we be consistently happy when our direct experiences of happiness are brief and transitory? Unfortunately, the causes of our unhappiness, mental and physical, lurk in the background of our lives, ready to manifest under the right circumstances. Is this existential situation inevitable and beyond our control? It is taught that we may liberate ourselves by looking deeply into the nature and causes of suffering.

Imagine yourself as a child lying in the grass in a woodland meadow. While gazing at the sky, view in wonderment the ever-changing cloud formations. Bring to mind a scene of sitting on a river bank or ocean beach watching the wave patterns constantly dying and renewing themselves in their ebb and flow. Recall witnessing unexpected changes in the circumstances of life and the despair of death. Reflecting on these experiences, we must conclude that impermanence or change is inherent in all situations.

How does this understanding relate to our existential situation, our stream of life experiences? Because we live in a constantly changing world, uncertainty is inevitable and arises in parallel with the subtle feeling of insecurity that underlies all relationships. Even the anticipation of change may bring a measure of anxiety, which may escalate into a feeling of dread. However, there is a positive side of change: seeds sprout; plants grow and yield harvest, and life refreshes itself and continues. Because things can change, it is possible to develop a sane relationship with the painful aspect of impermanence.

Individual freedom is a myth and an illusion because we are primarily imprisoned by our acquired personal and cultural conditioning. Thoughts and feelings are governed by deeply ingrained ego driven habit patterns from which our actions follow. Present circumstances and our relationship with others are foreshadowed by this conditioning. Witness the operation of our confusion, desires, hopes, and fears as we respond to the variety of life situations.

Attempting to escape perpetual boredom, we may get caught up in compulsive consumerism, addictive pursuits of pleasure, and obsessive forms of entertainment. The imposition of restrictive controls and regulations by parents or government officials leads to rebellion and violence. Even self-imposed minor compulsions such as wearing appropriate attire—fine linens to the temple, suit and tie to the office, or punk rags to school, cause resentments to fester and influence our behavior.

Spiritual ideals and aspirations may degenerate into a state of superficial satisfaction. A young woman wished to become a nun and serve God; however, having witnessed priestly improprieties, misogyny, and other hypocrisies, she felt betrayed and her faith was devastated. So, she became a corporate administrator and merely attended prominent churches on the Sabbath. A young man aspired to travel to India and become a religious ascetic or perhaps join the Peace Corps and give service to the sick and hungry; instead, he became sidetracked by the desire for money and the pleasures of the good life. He became a hedge fund manager and acquired a mansion in the suburbs.

To satisfy the desire for a deeper meaning of life, some of us may simply settle for a nominal membership in a church or temple. Or, we may feel drawn towards so-called spiritual groups and join an exotic religious sect or a fashionable cult movement. If these prove disappointing, our search for meaning may change to a rejection of all spiritual matters and result in our becoming a hedonic materialist. Loss of our original aspiration may degenerate into a generalized apathy towards the well-being of others. This attitude accommodates blind and deluded participation in destructive societal norms such as our collective failings in the stewardship of the planet, violent conflicts, apartheid, genocide, and a variety of perverted racial, economic, and class distinctions.

Nevertheless, there is a way out of our current existential dilemma. With meditation practice as the basis, the process of coming into relationship with our innate spirituality yields the fruits of meditation: altruism, love, clarity, peace, and well-being.

Meditation Session One

For one special moment, suspend normal activities and simply relax into being aware of your body and surroundings. No need to go to the temple or assume a meditation posture. Do not try to "meditate"; but just stop everything! This practice may be done while out walking or sitting wherever you are. Do not fixate on or label things, but just see, hear, and feel without judgement. End the session after a minute or so.

Looking and listening are normally directed at something and require willful effort. Here the idea is to make the subtle distinction with *seeing* and *hearing* as the pure play of effortless awareness wherein ego is not present.

Afterwards, reflect on your experience during that short session. Your mind was probably preoccupied with simply being aware, so there was no opportunity to generate thoughts of the past or future. Since there were no thoughts, there was no thinker, ego's grip was loosened. This was a mindfulness meditation practice. Repeat this practice throughout the day to ingrain the habit, keeping it short and alive.

Basic Cause of Our Dilemma

The primary cause of our existential situation stems from ego's self-cherishing and the associated thought and behavior habit patterns that may harm the wellbeing of ourselves and others. Its root is grasping and clinging, to illusory phenomena. All things, including the self, are none other than a set of dependent relationships to which we give a name. Like the rainbow, they have no intrinsic independent existence, nevertheless, we perceive them as solid and substantial and think they are real. This paradoxical concept of *no-self* will be thoroughly examined beginning with Chapter Eight, "Search for the Self."

Because of this basic ignorance, we may be caught in a web of anxiety or feeling of uncertainty. Imprisonment is accepted and endured in a matrix of confusion because our mind is too wild and untamed to understand the dilemma. Our self-image is deluded and maintained through the conditioning of habituated ego-clinging. Identifying with our own mindsets may lead to the formation of destructive opinions. Viewing others through the cataracts of memory, with its accumulated hurts and pleasures, makes it difficult to maintain freshness in relationships. Because of these mistaken views, our perceptions may become distorted and lead to biased thoughts and harmful actions. Thus begins our march into delusion.

All experiences, thoughts, and actions from this life as well as those from our past lives are recorded in our mind stream. Residues of these experiences, our karma, follow us like a shadow and are stored in our personal memory bank, like seeds ready to sprout at the appropriate time. The collective karma of society has also been absorbed by our consciousness and is stored in our karmic account. When conditions are right, this group karma becomes the causes that take root and give rise to our universal experience of isolation, tribalism, war, division, violence, sickness, and famine.

It is evident that sustaining real happiness or contentment requires a fresh approach—a new kind of intelligence. Happiness is somewhat equated with brief moments of pleasurable activities such as eating chocolate, watching a football game, lounging on the beach, or conversing with loved ones. Unfortunately, all of these micro-pleasures are short lived and may turn at any moment. We may gain weight from over-indulgence, our team may lose the game, we may get sunburned, or we may become caught up in the drama of conflict.

These pleasures are also relative as well as temporary. For those experiencing continuous poverty and fear, simply having small moments of relief from hunger and oppression is great happiness—like a fountain of cool water to parched lips. Others become dissatisfied with ordinary pleasures and seek happiness in the pursuit of extreme forms of gratification such as excessive indulgence in alcohol, drugs, or sexual misconduct. Satisfaction of these cravings yields the misery of addiction. As sung by Johnny Lee:

looking for love in all the wrong places

Regardless of our status of being powerful, rich, and beautiful or oppressed, poor, and ugly, dissatisfaction marks our life. Although one category has many more brief moments of meaningless pleasure, neither are truly happy; each merely experiences different degrees and modes of unhappiness. Ironically, the stress of the privileged mirrors the distress of the oppressed. In-between these extremes, most experience a subtle undercurrent of anxiety with occasional feelings of dread, loneliness, and insecurity.

We are attached to loved ones but separation occurs; we cling to possessions and pleasures but losses and pain occur. Energy and time are squandered by worrying and protecting the status quo, inevitably to no avail. Few escape the ever-present wake of chronic dissatisfaction in our stream of being. Most of us will experience the suffering of sickness and old age. All will meet death. Moments of joy and freedom from strife occur rarely, only to swiftly fade like last night's dream. Samsara, the perpetual carousel of life, spins merrily along. This is our existential situation continuously created and shared by beings on this planet.

Let us observe our feeling when involved in an act of spontaneous unselfishness with no desire for the warmth of recognition and credit. We may notice the selfless glow we feel when helping a lost child find its mother or nurturing a wounded bird? This experience of happiness, unlike the aforesaid pleasures, is clearly of a higher order. Its genuineness is a clue to the origin of the nature of real joy.

This scenario of suffering is neither our fundamental natural condition nor our preordained destiny. Facing the causes of suffering is our ultimate challenge—life's manifest task. On the surface, Nietzsche's view on suffering has some merit:

To live is to suffer; to survive is
to find some meaning in the suffering.

However, if we wish to go beyond mere survival, let us examine the nature of suffering, its causes, and its cessation. Moving from the darkness of ego's confusion into the clarity of knowing the true nature of self, a luminous quality arises within that enables us to benefit self and others. This, our *genesis trek*, is the path that engages the skillful means of meditation to look into the roots of our fundamental discontent and culminates in the radical awakening of the mind of compassion.

The Jewel Within

The Journey of Awakening

Know O' Seeker, there is a way out of the morass of chaos, the confusion that entraps many living beings in suffering and despair. Like disoriented wayfarers in a world on the brink of insanity, we may feel alienated in a foreign and inhospitable land— vulnerable to spiraling further into the heart of uncertainty. Our innate core status, *spirit,* is nurtured by the inherent benevolence of the universe and underlies the possibility of liberation from the misery of self-delusion. It is better to recognize or think of ourselves as divine souls rather than beings in possession of an appendage called a soul. From the swamp of ignorance, there is a high ground and a path of return to clarity and luminosity—a journey of awakening via meditation that continues life after life. Fortunately, sages graced with *robes of many colors* have provided signposts for such a journey.

The path of return to our primordial *source* of being—our mythical *Eden*, our natural home, leads to luminous clarity and liberation from our current existential status. Treading this path is a journey of discovery and radical transformation. It is a life-altering project for the dissatisfied and the disenchanted— weary ones who have known many dead-ends in their search for meaning. It connects with the womb of being wherein we may experience metamorphosis through the compassionate openness of meditation. This path leads to a generative spiritual practice—a process that refreshes the mind and deconstructs the obstacles to wellbeing.

The opening line of this section could well have been: "Know O' Wanderer, we are like a homeless orphan with no heritage—origin and identity unknown. Although we have a name, we are not that name." Both openings initiate the arduous journey to reclaim our royal birthright, moving to our natural primordial condition—the state of purity, freedom, and wholeness. Some say that outwardly we appear as a frog but that inwardly we are actually a prince or princess, ready to be liberated by the touch of love. Here, it is said that we are a Buddha-in-becoming, ready to awaken.

The essence of being, *spirit*, is innate to all living beings. Veiled by a mantle of ignorance, there is, nevertheless, that precious jewel within our heart which is self-secret because we do not recognize it. Sentient beings, from the smallest microbe to the largest mammal, desire happiness and want to be free from suffering. Acknowledgment of this simple observation forms the basis for sharing our common burden of uncertainty and dissatisfaction.

Fortunately for us, the human genus has the mental capacity to look into the causes of our predicament and the altruistic will to benefit others. Since animals do not have this capacity, they must depend on our kindness and compassion for their wellbeing. Within the collective karma of the human race, few are lucky enough to be born into spiritually nurturing circumstance such as: possessing a sound mind and body, a hospitable environment free of war and strife, adequate means of livelihood with leisure time, and access to educational and spiritual teachings.

Among these, rare are those who see the urgency or necessity to awaken from our dreamlike existence.

> *Once in a magic land of timeless time, the child of five or six years—pure of heart in that age of innocence, visited his grandmother. His favorite pastime was to explore the surrounding woods and stroll along the creek bank, frequently stopping to gather wild flowers for her. She always exhibited delight and surprise when he presented her with a colorful bouquet. From her core of being, joyfulness and grace came as blessings whose fragrance permeated their relationship. As the child perceived this deep connection, an inner flower of realization blossomed in his heart:*

Joys and sorrows of relationship,
intimately experienced,
are shared by all.
Profound interconnections
formed in past lives,
carry over to the present.
Truly, all beings
have been my most precious loved one
many, many times.

The attainment of happiness and freedom from suffering for all beings can become our noble mandate and motive for action. From this perspective of interconnectivity, we may cultivate a mind of compassionate openness and the wish to remove the obstacles to wellbeing.

Imagine that the treasure we wish for, the jewel of enlightenment, is hidden at the top of a distant mountain. To seek the jewel, virtuous qualities are required for the journey. Ordinary qualities are not sufficient because they divert our search into the wanderings of samsara, the indefinitely repeated cycles of birth, death, and rebirth caused by karma. To prepare, we may simply appreciate the beauty of the idea that meditation is integral to a virtuous life. Our motives will gradually gestate into the certainty of pure aspirations and requisite virtuous qualities will unfold and ripen into skillful means.

To shed light on some aspects of this journey, let us look into the mental processes that occur after a typical dream. Immediately on waking, before the regular activities of our mind set in, vivid emotions, palpable and intense, may linger. They are the surreal offspring of the remembrance of the dream. However, the realization that the people and activities in the dream were not substantive but simply illusions quickly intrudes on our reverie. These were mirage-like reappearances of karmic memories and soon disappear into the realm of memory remnants. Analogous to recognizing the illusory nature of our dreams, the flame of meditation exposes and purifies our hidden delusions and mental habit patterns while we are awake. This profound experience of meditative consciousness relates to the ordinary waking state as the ordinary waking state relates to dreaming.

Our journey of awakening is purposed to disrupt ego's drama by addressing the karmic residues of consciousness which impede our radical transformation. This process involves transcending our ego cherishing. Understanding and insight do not come from accumulated knowledge or concepts but from the direct perception of reality through meditation. Let us set aside preconceived notions and start the process of inquiry from the stance of not-knowing, like an empty vase—receptive, without expectations.

Throughout history, special teachers have left guidance and maps applicable to our journey. Tradition records that during a span of forty years, the Buddha gave eighty-four thousand dharma teachings in recognition of the diversity of human minds. Jesus the Christ gave the Sermon on the Mount and the Beatitudes to the multitudes. During this journey, we will encounter requisite teachings suitable for each and every temperament. Our approach to meditation will be both passionate and tentative. Communion with the sources will be respectful; however, no traditions are immune to the light of inquiry. Let us step into the baptismal waters of the meditation practice river with the confidence that enlightenment is beyond the other shore.

Dawn Breaking

Why Meditation?

When embarking on the spiritual search, we may be drawn towards a symbol of that which is beyond our reach. The silhouette of a distant mountain top, shrouded in mystery, framed in the dawn of a rising sun, beckons with hidden promise. It holds in trust a secret and sacred jewel of meaning. Our inquiry into meditation approaches this mountain, the way to which is obscured by the mist of unknowing. There are ways of cutting through obstacles and breaking out of our chrysalis of self-absorption and entering the clear light. The caterpillar is instinctively compelled to find a quiet place to begin its process of pupal envelopment. But it is only after it dissolves itself and sheds the cocoon that the glorious butterfly emerges. We too must dissolve our ego-clinging and shed our self-cherishing to liberate the luminous nature of our mind.

The mirror of meditation will be applied to peer into perennial questions: "Who am I?" "What is the nature of my relationship as the meditator to meditation?" "What is the role of listening and studying, followed by reflection and action in my quest?" These activities are within the realm of thought and time; yet, "Is not meditation beyond thought and time?" "Is a 'system of meditation' a trick of the conditioned mind, another conundrum?" "Is there a way of preparing the field of my mind and heart that will enable the right receptivity for meditation?" Meditation practice facilitates the process of empowering a totally different kind of intelligence, free of conditioning, to naturally arise. The seed of this new intelligence is conceived and nurtured in the womb of meditation.

To approach these questions, perennial wisdom teachings affirm there is a way. A personal and intimate relationship with meditation is its key feature. A proper reception for the teachings is an open mind—the essential condition for hearing and communing with truth. Study and reflection provide understanding at the level of intellect and meditation practice deepens it into the continuum of heart and mind. The grace of meditation then marks our mode of appearance in the world.

Meditation is a rare state of consciousness primarily concerned with the process of naked awareness rather than the contents of thoughts and memories. It has been given many names such as: "samadhi," "trance," "rapture," and "enlightenment." Meditation—delicate and ephemeral, is like a humming bird hovering nearby, tantalizing and immune to grasping. Approaching tentatively with loving confidence brings joyful engagement.

Like developing a masterpiece of music or painting, meditation practice relies on unfolding inner qualities of love and compassion to achieve clarity. Masterpieces are distinguished by their transcendent qualities beyond the applications of mundane skills. Pertinent qualities will be nurtured throughout our journey. As an art, meditation cannot be taught; nevertheless, its practice can be learned. From the power of Beethoven's passionate love and practice of music, his inner listening flowered into the creation of a sonata. Similarly, our meditation practice can yield the sacred fruit of luminosity. The art of meditation practice is our most important vocation. Just as the breath is fundamental to the sustenance of our body, meditation is vital to the nourishment of our spirit. Meditation practice is the sword that pierces the veil of self delusion and loosens our attachment to ego driven concepts. It clears the clouds of poisonous emotions and blesses us with the direct perception of reality.

Meditation is a transcendental yet natural experience of being fully awake in pristine awareness wherein the world is recognized as it is in its primordial purity. It is beyond the limitations of conditioned conceptual mind. Perhaps we have come close to the experience of meditation in one of those rare moments when our mind abided calmly. Attention was totally present as the self slept in the background. Meditation may have taken the form of an insight beyond thought or an ecstatic feeling of joyousness beyond pleasure—like unexpectedly coming upon the vista of a rainbow. It momentarily graces us with its presence before dissolving back into the empty sky. Its beauty lingers as a fleeting afterglow of gratitude.

Transcending the complicity of ego cherishing and concept clinging, the truth born of meditation is inherently genuine. If we come upon a truth, we may marvel at its beauty and profundity; but unless it becomes our ground of being, it is merely cosmetic. Our journey culminates with immersion into the authenticity of our own insights—the true baptism of fire that transforms our mind and heart.

Meditation Session Two

The object chosen for this more traditional mindfulness practice is our breath. In a quiet place, let us sit up straight in a meditation posture and relax our body and mind. We may now observe our breathing process as the breath moves gently through the nose and slightly opened mouth. Practicing this way for two or three minutes each session is sufficient in the beginning.

If we become distracted or lose focus, we may simply relax and return to sensing our breath. Noticing the distraction is beneficial because it shows that our mindfulness practice is working.

As this practice matures we may observe thoughts as they arise. Where did they come from? Where do they abide? Where do they go? These questions will become the fodder for a deeper insight meditation practice.

Why the Buddha Path?

A Western method of approaching the spectrum of ways to enlightenment is to study and reflect on the views of saints and sages representative of philosophy, theosophy, esotericism, and religion. This book explores the path to truth and liberation by entering the light of the Buddha's dharma teachings on the nature of reality. We will not follow a religious path because Buddhism is not, in fact, a religion since there are no supernatural elements in its practice. The Buddha was not a Buddhist, he was a rather extraordinary human who discovered a jewel of sublime truth and resolved to share it.

Two and a half millennia ago, in the northern part of India near the Himalayas, a prince was born to the queen and king of a small country. The king received an omen that this child was special and destined to become a teacher or holy man. Naturally, the father wanted his son to continue the royal lineage and follow him as king. So he devised a cage of material and psychological protection around the boy. Confining him to a great palace—surrounded by vast gardens and lakes—with attendants catering to all his wants, the plan seemed to be working. The king was quite happy when his son married a beautiful princess and had a wonderful child. Nevertheless, an inevitable restlessness grew in the mind of the prince, so early one morning he had his most trusted attendant saddle his horse. He surreptitiously left the confines of the palace to explore the outside world and proceeded towards a nearby village. Almost immediately, on both sides of the road, he encountered squalid little huts, each with several inhabitants. Many of the people appeared sick and miserable. A crippled old woman approached him and asked for food. He gave her what he had and continued his exploration. On the side of the road, in a ditch, he came upon a dead person covered with flies and vermin. Overwhelmed by these experiences of poverty, sickness, old age, and death, unbearable compassion arose in his heart. He was determined to find a way to end the suffering of all beings. He left everything behind and became a wandering ascetic until he realized that was not the right way. He ultimately resolved to sit and meditate under the Bodhi tree and not leave until he understood the true nature of reality. Thus was his journey of awakening and attainment of full enlightenment. He became the Buddha, the enlightened one. We too may become liberated through the insights and teachings he eventually shared after his awakening.

Why rely on the Buddha's teachings? A long lineage of sages bear testament to his sane and scientific approach to dealing with the human condition. They directly recorded his teachings in writing and cross checked them with the memories of other hearers. Confidence is enhanced by the Buddha extolling the importance of questioning all teachings (especially his) and accepting none with blind faith. Even if we believe in the truth of a particular concept, nevertheless, it should be held tentatively and not considered to be the final word.

The Buddha taught that we should do no harm and to use ourselves as an example on how to treat others. Sages and religious figures throughout history have universally advocated this "golden rule" of harmlessness and virtue.

Many of the teachings given by the Buddha remain quite unique such as:

- We can tame our own mind.
- We are our own savior and master.
- Men and women have equal capacity to attain enlightenment and teach the dharma.
- We can know the truth of suffering.
- We can know the truth of delusion - that whatever we perceive or think, is not valid or absolute because things change.

A most compelling reason to trust the Buddha's teachings is his display of compassion for the suffering of others. Although he had achieved freedom from suffering for himself, he had doubts about sharing his insights with others. Upon leaving the Bodhi tree, he expressed:

I have found a truth that is profound, peaceful,
free from extremes, luminous, uncompounded, like a nectar.
But no matter to whom I utter this, people will not hear.
Therefore, I shall remain in the forest without speaking.

Nevertheless, he decided to try and teach. Many Buddhists consider this to be the Buddha's first teaching. His reluctance to speak is based on his view that the truth of our life, of phenomena, of reality cannot be defined, conceptualized, verbalized, or symbolized. All these attempts are limiting. Words themselves are mere symbols or pointers that easily transform into useless concepts and platitudes unless we have personally discovered the truth within. Let us be open-minded and carefully examine the teachings and the teacher. After a measure of confidence in the teachings and faith in the teacher has been established, we should still hold our truths lightly until certainty arises. Verification of this certainty is affirmed by the way we live and relate to others.

Approaching Meditation Practice

If our mind was as calm and clear as a still forest pool, there would be no need to practice meditation. Unfortunately, most of our minds are like a "monkey-mind," conditioned to be hyper-occupied by chasing thoughts of the past or bouncing off plans for the future. Various disturbing emotions arise continuously, clinging to them leads to confusion and anxiety. Hence, there is the need to train our mind to bring it to a stable state of calmness and clarity.

Let us orient ourselves to the meditation practice sessions by simply placing our body into a comfortable position, relaxing our mind into a quiet mode, and observing the natural breathing process. Be aware of the associated tactile sensations. Some favor feeling the diaphragm rising and falling. Some are more attuned to the cool sensation of the breath over the lips, to the feeling of a gentle breeze through the nose, or to its sound like the wind playing in trees. Settle in with the natural rhythm of the breathing process.

The meditation practice sessions are progressive and sequentially designed to be repeated until we feel ready to proceed to the next. Consistent regular practice at a convenient time and place establishes a natural daily habit pattern. Even one minute each morning or evening is productive practice. Prolonging a session until discouragement and fatigue come into play is counterproductive. Allowing aching sit-bones to escalate into distraction violates common sense. In this context, one purpose of the practice is for body and mind to learn to be at ease with each other. Hence: short sessions, many times are recommended.

In the early stages of practice, our mind seems to be chattering like a flock of excited birds. We may feel that the door of our unconscious has been left open. Actually, the proliferation of thoughts and emotions was present all along; we just weren't aware of the cacophony. We have no need to become involved or entangled with them and may simply allow the thoughts to disappear into oblivion like bubbles rushing to the top of a glass of champagne. There is no value in repressing thoughts nor chastising ourselves; we should just let them be and return to our meditation practice. As experience is gained, we may consider incorporating some of the features of the following "Traditional Meditation Protocol" .

Sitting Meditation

Traditional Meditation Protocol

The purpose of meditation practice is to remove the obstacles to knowing the truth so that we may free ourselves and all beings from suffering and lead the way to happiness. Feeling relaxed and at ease with no induced tensions in our body and mind are crucial to initiate the meditation practice session.

We may set the stage for the practice by acknowledging our motivation to benefit all beings. A secular person may reflect on their good fortune in having the opportunity and capacity to practice. A religious person may voice an opening prayer expressing thanksgiving and faith. This initial action creates a special ambience and invites the benevolent forces of nature to participate.

The following specific techniques are based on Shakyamuni Buddha's teachings and confirmed by twenty five centuries of empirical practice evidence. They are intended to provide efficient guidance for the serious meditation practitioner.

> 1. Select a regular time for practice based on personal circumstances. Find a suitable location relatively free of distractions that allows us to sit in privacy. Ideally we may go to a mountain top or a deep forest glade; however, a bathroom may be the most favorable.
>
> 2. Assume an upright sitting posture. Imagine a cord attached to the crown of the head, suspending the spinal column. This

position helps coordinate the breathing process with the flow of subtle body energies through specialized inner channels. Release all bodily and mental tensions and settle into a relaxed, natural alignment. Alternatively, we may lie on our back, but that may induce drowsiness.

3. Use a firm cushion for support when sitting on the floor in a cross-legged position. The pelvis should be tilted slightly forward with the knees touching the floor. Alternatively, we may sit upright on a chair with uncrossed legs and feet on the floor. It may help to place books under the rear chair legs to obtain a slight forward tilt.

4. Rest cupped hands in the lap, traditionally right over left with thumb tips touching; alternatively, place the hands on the knees with palms down.

5. Position elbows slightly away from the body like a vulture airing its wings.

6. Tilt the chin down and slightly open the mouth, letting the tip of the tongue touch or float freely near the palate to mitigate swallowing.

7. Partially open the eyes without their movement, look into the empty space "an arrow's length" in front. Allow the eyelids to blink naturally as they will. Without focusing on a central point, assume a wide angle panoramic view. If sitting on a mountaintop, gaze into the vast blue sky. Keeping the eyes

(and other sense gates) open serves to transition the meditation practice into our daily life. However, it is ok to close the eyes if visual objects become too distracting.

We may seal the practice by closing each session with an expression of generosity and gratitude. Project the wish that others may also benefit from our practice. Elevate the energy in your environment by sharing harmonious feelings experienced at this time. A religious person may feel that a healing prayer will be readily heard at this point and wish to share the benediction from that perspective. These closing actions are meritorious because they multiply the effect of the practice.

Meditation Session Three

The object of this mindfulness practice is to look separately at each of the first three of the Buddha's *four foundations of mindfulness*, which will be discussed in Chapter Four. For this and subsequent meditation sessions, it's best to sit up straight.

1. Body – Scan each body part from the top of your head to the tips of your toes. Note the tactile sensations of each part. Are the sensations fixed or do they change with time?

2. Feelings – While sitting, be aware of feelings that arise. Do they elicit pleasure, pain, or neutral responses? Does your itching knee feel unpleasant or is it your mind that feels?

3. Mind – Observe the state of your mind. In particular, notice if the mind is involved: with greed or not; with malice or not; with delusion or not; and with dullness or not.

Close the session by resting mindfully.

Chapter Two

Preparing the Garden of Meditation

Meditation is like the subtle, fleeting fragrance of a newly opened flower bud. It cannot be touched or seen directly but may be uniquely sensed and thereby becomes integral with our consciousness. The practice of meditation has prerequisites analogous to those required for growing flowers from seeds. The virgin field of our mind is to be readied for a profound conception to occur in this garden. The weeds of self-centeredness are to be rooted out. Seeds of noble aspirations of loving-kindness are to be sown. Plants nurtured in the garden of meditation are precious and perennial for as given in Genesis 1:11 they are as:

fruit trees bearing fruit
that carries its own seed.

Guidelines From Perennial Sages

Virtuous qualities are a universal hallmark of the spiritual quest. Cultivation of these profound traits is essential to fully connect with the process of meditation. Sages and religious traditions advocate special requirements for approaching the Divine.

Through Moses came the Ten Commandments giving rules of conduct. From Psalms 46:10:

Be still and know that I am God.

In his Sermon on the Mount, Jesus proclaimed:

Blessed are the pure in heart
For they shall see God.

To surrender to the Divine Will, the Prophet Muhammad categorically advocated

the Great inner jihad.

His preeminent teaching was oriented towards an internal, individual, and spiritual struggle for self-improvement and personal moral purification.

From his insight into Sufism, the esoteric dimension of Islam, the representative poet and mystic, Rumi, says:

Whether you love the One

or another human being,
If you love enough,
in the end you will come into the
Presence of Love itself.

Helena the Theosophist urges aspirants to climb the golden stairs:

A Clean life,
an Open mind,
and a Pure heart,
attain to the temple of
Divine wisdom.

She affirms the existence of an *Ageless Wisdom* that informs the esoteric basis for the world's major religions.

The Chinese sage Lao Tzu says to those who wish to follow the Tao:

Like a lake without winds,
One must have a heart that is calm and quiet,
With great depth beneath it.
The Tao that can be expressed is not
the Eternal Tao.
Nevertheless, something there is,
formless yet complete.
In the beginning it existed.
Its name is not known,
But it is called Tao.
It is the Mystery of Mysteries.

From the Confucian sage, Mencius:

Try your best to treat others as you would wish
To be treated yourself,
And you will find that this
Is the shortest way to goodness.

From a Jain prayer:

Friendship to all living forms,
Delight in the qualities of the virtuous ones,
Unlimited compassion for all suffering beings,
Equanimity towards all who wish me harm,
May my soul have these dispositions
now and forever.

From the Sikh sacred scriptures (Adi Granth):

The One God pervades all:
And seeing Him,
I am wholly in bloom.

The Shinto approaches the *Divine* heart of truth

Through sincerity,
A pure heart,
And uprightness.

The Hindu sage Patanjali gave spiritual guidelines to attain the *meditative* state of mind. These emphasize:

Abstaining from harmful behavior and
cultivating generosity and devotion.

The dharma teachings of Gautama Buddha, the Enlightened One, are summarized in his *Noble Eightfold Path* and

lead to the wisdom of compassion
and liberation from suffering
for all beings.

These imperatives universally embody the truth that negative qualities cause suffering and a virtuous mind generates happiness. They are essential to our inquiry and furnish the requisite seeds to be sown in the garden of meditation. Plants harvested here will bear the fruit that benefits ourselves and others. Let us take to heart Jesus's "Parable of the Sower" and give great care in preparing this garden. Early in this process, having recognized and grown weary of our life drama and its entanglements, a warrior-like fearlessness will emerge.

Mental Afflictions

Impeding our journey are three major poisons that afflict our mind: Delusion, Attachment, and Anger. There are also three derivative poisons: Greed, Jealousy, and Envy. These mental obstructions are the immediate causes of our discontent.

1. Delusion is not recognizing the real nature of phenomena and ourselves. Without discriminating wisdom, we sink into the muck of ignorance wherein noxious seeds take root and sprout within our consciousness. These offspring masquerade in attractive guise and rarely appear as ugly or malodorous weeds. Witness our gullibility when confronted with charismatic politicians' contagious lies and the news media's self-serving sensationalism and misinformation. We feel helpless in the face of the greedy and powerful government lobbyists. Exploitations of our delusion by the entertainment media panders to our baser fantasies and the advertisement industry's clever solicitations trigger unrestrained consumerism. Underlying these mundane delusions is our sense of separateness from others, the greatest delusion—viewing our existence as an independent self.

Our conditioned self-image is like a case of mistaken identity. Are we certain of who we really are, deep in our heart? Could we be a potential thief? If we were poor and hungry, would we steal food for our family? Are we capable of killing? If we saw a loved one being brutally murdered, would we want to kill the killer? Are we a liar? If we were a politician running for office, would we cheat to achieve our goal for the greater good of our country? If we were born into fortunate circumstances and have never known poverty, conflict, and temptation, is it certain that we are free of selfishness, greed, racism, violence, and immorality?

2. Attachment reveals itself as excessive desire in the form of obsessive longing to gain attractive things or as possessive love for my spouse, my opinions, and especially my self. Resistance to examining cherished beliefs guards our attachment to ego. Since we are our religious beliefs, we fear the light of scrutiny may deconstruct our sense of identity. We are so attached to outcomes that we become upset if things don't go our way. If our candidate loses the election, we and our country will suffer greatly. We are very reluctant to change our mind about liking or disliking anything because we are so comfortable with our delusions.

3. Anger is a most destructive force in our relationship with others. Feeling annoyed, impatient, or resentful are pernicious forms of anger. The effects of malice, the offspring of anger, range from estrangement to violence and outright war.

4. Greed is seen in its grossest form as the excessive accumulation of and reluctance to share our wealth with others. A subtle form of disguised greed is seeking praise or gratitude for apparently generous deeds. A rich person may donate a fortune to a charitable foundation but also wants their name emblazoned. They also want a tax deduction.

5. Jealousy is a combination of delusion, anger, and attachment. It manifests as paranoia, feelings of rage, and anxiety or fear of loss. Conditional love for another gives rise to the drama of jealousy. Real love is unconditional and its primary concern is happiness for the other.

6. Envy is a combination of the same three poisons as jealousy, but with a higher proportion of greed and attachment. We feel discontent because we don't have the good looks, intelligence, fine home, or fancy car of our co-worker. Envy's persona shows itself when there is a lack of feeling empathetic joy for the good fortune of another.

The seeds of these afflictions must be culled and burnt prior to the final harvest; otherwise, their spawn will continue to obstruct our liberation. Life involved in the constant pursuit of pleasure or power is hollow and devoid of meaning, always in the shadow of dissatisfaction. Successes are enjoyed but failures may follow. Security is not guaranteed and fulfillment is never enough. Personal relationships are chronically tainted with disagreements. The ebb and flow of nice sounding words become contrived and joyless. Indifference to the suffering of those outside our circle may lead to hardening of the arteries of compassion. Awareness of these observations informs and supports our motivation for undertaking this journey.

Three Poisons

Delusion reined and Ego was king.
With arrogant heart and mind gone awry,
Ignorance ruled and love departed, from me.

I saw the truth, laughter began.
I cried with joy, love's here again.
It found its space, where blooms the grace of,
Hallelujah!
Hallelujah! Hallelujah!
Hallelujah! Hallelujah!

My heart beat fast and my face turned red,
With throat on fire and eyes filled with tears,
Anger was there and love departed, from me.

I saw the truth, laughter began.
I cried with joy, love's here again.
It found its space, where blooms the grace of,
Hallelujah!
Hallelujah! Hallelujah!
Hallelujah! Hallelujah!

Desire burst forth and I wanted all,
With trembling voice and passion rising,
Greed overwhelmed and love departed, from me.

I saw the truth, laughter began.

I cried with joy, love's here again.
It found its space, where blooms the grace of,
Hallelujah!
Hallelujah! Hallelujah!
Hallelujah! Hallelujah!

[When voiced to the tune of Cohen's *"Hallelujah"*, this is a musical meditation.]

Virtuous Qualities

Two and a half millennia ago, the Buddha taught the *great perfections* (Skt., *paramitas*), which, when perfected, uniquely mark a fully enlightened being. We may practice these six modes of behavior as a spiritual path to empower us to truly benefit all beings. They will bloom into a display of benevolence as our meditation practice deepens. The six paramitas are: Generosity, Discipline, Patience, Enthusiasm, Mindfulness, and Wisdom.

1. Generosity is the quality of being kind and open-hearted. There are three kinds of generosity: directly sharing our material wealth with those in need. Wise ones say that the seeds of generosity are inherently present within each of us. Witness a young child's joyful natural behavior when sharing candy with playmates. Because generosity is innate, these seeds can be nurtured and sprouted by training.

A second kind of generosity is giving protection from fear. Mothers naturally give this to their babies as do fathers to their family. First class governments protect their citizens through health care, living assistance, and educational opportunity.

Third, and the greatest generosity, is to share spiritual teachings to the extent we are capable. Leading by example, most of us can teach a child about kindness and forgiveness. If we know more than another about the dharma, is it not our duty to share it?

What to do with the obvious fact that sometimes we are not generous? Let us germinate the seeds of generosity by giving away small possessions with no sense of pride or reluctance. Gradually, there will be no sense of reservation when giving away prized possessions. We may develop the habit of seeking out a homeless person to give food or money. Personally handing a gift to someone is more beneficial than mailing a check to a charitable institution. Obsessing that this gesture may foster laziness or enable addictions will cause us to discount the value of generosity. This may lead us to stray from the path and become lost in the morass of greed. Let us be grateful for our good fortune that makes giving possible.

2. Discipline is following right ethics and moral conduct. This also has three aspects. First is to do no harm. Similar to the ethic embodied in the Hippocratic Oath we resolve to never hurt any sentient being: human, animal, or Gaia.

A second aspect is to do virtuous actions that benefit others. Thus, karmic merit is accumulated in our life savings account.

Third is to take care of ourselves by cultivating virtue and practicing the dharma teachings on meditation. This grows the self-esteem that brings happiness and well-being to those around us.

3. Patience elegantly and skillfully attenuates anger and forestalls the arising of malice. It prevents the escalation of malevolent situations which, ironically, we may have created. Patience calms by allowing time and

space for the fangs of malice to withdraw. We may cultivate an attitude of forbearance towards the faults of others as well as our own problematic dramas. Jesus taught: "Love your enemy and judge not others." Attend carefully to this precept because many of us have professed this for two thousand years and still haven't got it.

4. Enthusiasm refers to a joyful and diligent attentiveness that is constantly mindful of the actions of our body, speech, and mind. Let us diligently protect our body from injury due to harmful drugs, unhealthy foods, hazardous occupations, and neglect of nurturing rest. We may allow our speech to become pleasant and non-injurious and our mind to become calm and clear. Let us take delight in wholesome actions and joyfully practice the dharma without procrastination.

5, Mindfulness refers to the quality of being calm, clear, and perceptive. Being aware of the action of speech, we tend to not lie, gossip, or slander. Mindful awareness leads us to speak kindly to and of others. Accomplishing this paramita leads to a mind of serenity, like a still forest pool capable of reflecting perfectly. This prepares the mind to be receptive to the truth born of wisdom.

6. Wisdom sees into the destructive effects of the mental afflictions such as maintaining wrong views, obsessively craving desirable things, and indulging in hatred towards others. When perfected, this virtue

exhibits loving kindness, vast compassion, and transcendental awareness. Stabilizing the mind through the practice of mindfulness and insight meditation allows us to look into the nature of mind itself and to see things as they really are. On attaining full realization we can truly benefit others as well as ourselves.

The quality of generosity is particularly relevant to accomplishing our journey, for it prevents the constant stumbling and tripping over ego. Purification in the fountain of a generous heart is the preeminent qualification to begin right meditation practice. This action lightens our burden of ego-cherishing.

At our core we are a spiritual being; therefore, virtuousness is an innate part of our nature and can be unfolded, nurtured, and manifested. Virtue doesn't arise from nothing; it is latent as a seed within us. The four ghosts in Dickens' novel *A Christmas Carol* were able to transform the miser, Scrooge, into a generous philanthropist because the seed of generosity was present in his heart.

Practicing the paramitas unfolds natural virtues and is analogous to filling our magical storehouse, our personal memory bank, with the seeds of transformation. This is not so much an act of accumulating but a process of deconstructing regressive habit patterns and making space for innate virtue to express itself. Although seemingly fabricated at first, with practice they become integral and manifest as the *Four Immeasurables*. With a wrong motive, fabricated virtues may become disguised forms of greed and self-aggrandizement or lead to complacency and self-satisfaction. The ambition to acquire virtue as a pious possession prevents us from harvesting it for the benefit of others. One whose motives arise out of profound compassion and the pure wish to help others, then chooses the path to enlightenment is called a bodhisattva (Skt., *bodhisattva*). The great perfections arise when the narcissistic notion of self is abandoned—the ultimate sacrifice to spirit.

Long ago, during the fourth century CE, in a small Indian village, there lived a devout monk named Arya Asanga. He was obsessed with the wish to see the Buddha, so he left the monastery and went into solitary retreat in the mountains. There, through his diligence in practice, he hoped to connect with the Buddha. However, after practicing meditation for twelve years with no apparent success in attaining his goal, he became discouraged and decided to give up the retreat and return to his village. Along the way back, he chanced upon a bitch lying by the side of the road. She was emaciated, her hindquarters rotting and covered with maggots. Experiencing excruciating pain, she growled and tried to bite anyone who came near. Asanga was conflicted with fear and an unbearable feeling of compassion. Nevertheless, he cut a piece of flesh off his own body and fed it to the starving beast. He then began to use a stick to remove the maggots but realized that would hurt them and that the only safe way would be to use his tongue. Asanga got down on his knees but was so repulsed by the rotting, writhing mass that he closed his eyes. Nevertheless, he stuck out his tongue to begin removing the maggots but only felt the ground. When he opened his eyes, the dog was gone; there in its place was the Buddha he sought. His twelve years of practice had dissolved his negative karma and obscurations sufficiently to see the dog's suffering. His compassion and kindness enabled him to see the Buddha.

Four Immeasurables

Unlike development of the six paramitas which requires deliberate cultivation, there are four sublime aspirations that naturally and effortlessly emerge in parallel with the paramitas, like the fragrance of flowers permeating the garden. Through our practice, we too may enjoy their unfoldment. Traditionally known as the Four Immeasurables, they are: Loving kindness, Compassion, Joy, and Equanimity.

1. Loving kindness is the extension of unlimited, universal good will to all beings without discrimination, including the wish that they be happy and obtain the causes and conditions of happiness.
2. Compassion is the boundless wish that all beings be free from suffering and the causes and conditions of suffering.
3. Joy is the unbridled empathetic delight in the success, welfare, and happiness of all beings.
4. Equanimity is the universal sense of even-mindedness and impartiality toward all beings— friends and enemies alike, in all the vicissitudes of life.

Compassion and karma may manifest in many different forms. Witness the story of Androcles, a Greek slave who escaped from his Roman master and ran away into the forest. While hiding beneath some fallen branches he heard the roar of an approaching lion. As it came into view, the lion was moaning in pain, raising his swollen and bleeding right paw imbedded with a large jagged thorn. Almost overcome with fear, Androcles, nevertheless, approached the lion and proceeded to carefully remove the thorn. Both of them laid down to rest together for the night. At dawn some Roman soldiers came upon them. They tried to run away but Androcles and the lion were captured and returned to their prisons. Years later, as punishment for trying to escape again, Androcles was put in the arena to be killed by lions as sport for the emperor. When the gate to his cage was opened, the solitary lion charged, growling furiously. Suddenly he came to an abrupt stop. He recognized Androcles and raised his magnificent right paw and began to purr and nuzzle him—the natural karmic result of compassionate action.

Meditation Session Four

The object of this mindfulness practice is the contemplation of phenomena or mental formations, the fourth of the Buddha's Four Foundations of Mindfulness. This category includes the five obstacles to enlightenment: hedonic fixation (sensual desire), malice (ill will), laxity (dullness), excitation (anxiety), and uncertainty (doubt). Look carefully within and encourage one of these obstacles to present itself. When it appears clearly, let it come into full blossom. What happens when you directly face it without modification or improvement? Does it remain or fade away?

Communion

Chapter Three

Meditation and Love

Is there an intimate relationship between meditation and love or devotion? The word "devotion" mean to consecrate or make sacred and often refers to religious worship of a deity. It may also encompass love and commitment to spiritual teachings. If love is a golden coin, then one side is compassion and the other side is devotion. Devotion opens our heart to receive blessings from the teacher and the dharma.

The word "love" has many usages, some of which veil deeper meanings. It ranges from emotional attachment and affection for a person or object to an all-encompassing feeling of union with the *Divine*. The Abrahamic religions teach that *"God is Love."* This latter sense conveys an attitude of attunement that is universally beneficent. Ineffable love is approached through surrender of one's self. Then only may the power of devotion manifest as communion with an aspect of meditation.

Witness the example of Brother Lawrence and his experience of devotion. He was an uneducated footman prior to becoming a lay brother among the barefoot Christian Carmelites. His conversion was the result of his relation to a "dry and leafless tree standing gaunt against the snow." He contemplated deeply the new life promised by the coming spring. From that moment on, he blossomed forth in communion with *Love,* endeavoring "to walk as in *Love* 's presence."

Excerpts from a letter to his priest convey a sense of abiding devotion while he was engaged in mundane duties and formal periods of prayer or contemplation. Brother Lawrence exposes his heart thusly:

And I make it my business
Only to persevere in Love's holy presence,
Wherein I keep myself by a simple attention,
and a general fond regard to Love,
Which I may call an actual presence of Love, or better,
an habitual, silent, and secret conversation with Love,
which causes me Joys and Raptures
Inwardly and outwardly.

Then with ingenuous humility:

I consider myself as the most wretched of men
Who has committed all sorts of crimes
against his King.
Touched with a sensible regret,
I confess to Him all my wickedness,
and ask His forgiveness.
I abandon myself in His hands
that He may do what He wishes with me.
My King, full of mercy and goodness,
Very far from chastising me,
Embraces me with love.
Thus am I from time to time in
His holy presence.

And the internal sensation when he applies himself to prayer:

I feel all my spirit and all my soul lift itself up
without any care or effort of mine.
It continues as it were
suspended and firmly fixed in Love,
In its center and place of rest.

Finally, the soul's desire:

I cannot bear that this should be called delusion,
Because the soul which thus enjoys Love
Desires nothing but Love.
If this be delusion in me,
It belongs to Love to remedy it.

This example from the Christian tradition intimately illustrates the power of devotion to open our heart to the ineffable beyond concepts.

St. John of the Cross in his *Dark Night of the Soul* speaks of a meditation that brings an inner peace. "This peace—so delicate and subtle —does its work in stillness and solitude. [It] begins to come through pure spirit, through simple contemplation, untainted by discursive thought." Referring to the infused contemplation, he says: "Contemplation is nothing other than a secret, peaceful, loving inflow of [the ineffable]. If given room, it will fire the soul in the spirit of love."

From the tradition of Islam, Sufis emphasize a devotional approach to the ineffable, the very essence of love and light. The Sufi Saint and poet, Rumi, embraces the highest form of this love as the path to the divine. He expresses this mystical devotion in verse:

O my soul, I searched from end to end:
I saw in thee naught save the Beloved;
Call me not infidel, O my soul,
if I say that thou thyself art He.
Ye who search of God, of God, pursue.
Ye need not search for God is you, is you!
Why seek ye something that was missing ne'er?
Save you, none is,
but you are—where, oh, where?

The Muslim Saint and Sufi mystic of the eighth century, Rabia Al Basra, embodied this passionate devotion and love. She famously declared, "I want to pour water into Hell and set fire to Paradise so that these two veils disappear and nobody worships [the ineffable] out of fear of Hell or hope for Paradise, but only for the sake of eternal beauty."

The Hindu scholar of the third century BCE, Patanjali, considered devotion to be one of the necessary preliminary practices leading to meditative integration. It involves self-sacrifice and helps to unite our conditioned consciousness with pure awareness. Paraphrasing from the *Bhagavad-Gita*:

When the yogi's attention is fixed on the Beloved,
Free from hope or fear or desire,
Then is one said to be harmonized.

As a lamp sheltered from the wind does not flicker,
Just so is the yogi of subdued mind
Absorbed in devotion to the Beloved.

In his book *Self-Realization through Love*, the eminent theosophist Dr. I. K. Taimni notes two stages on the Hindu path of devotion. The first stage involves constant effort and self-discipline to prepare and purify oneself for the expression of devotion. The second stage is reached when the aspirant has the experience in which *love* wells up from within naturally, constantly, and effortlessly. This is the direct awareness of reality.

The paramitas taught by the Buddha are grounded in love and compassion. The practice of generosity graces the endeavor of meditation with love and gratitude. The attainment of wisdom—the fruit of meditation—provides the insight to truly benefit ourselves and others. If trace elements of unconditional love and compassion for the suffering of all beings are not present in the soil of our heart, then our practice will be barren and its potential harvest will wither and dry.

The connection between devotion and meditation yields the epiphany of love. Perennial wisdom teaches that the paths of devotion and meditation ultimately merge. The suggested first step of our practice sessions, "setting the stage," generates a special ambience to facilitate this merger. Empathizing with the inner state of these mystics enables us to receive their blessings and empowers our meditation. Devotion renders gratitude palpable so that we may feel open, receptive, joyous, and selfless. These four:

openness, receptivity, joyfulness, and no self-cherishing invite us to enter the sanctuary of our innermost being.

The following Coda, composed of traditional Buddhist elements, is a particular form of prayer or contemplation that expresses the wish that all sentient beings be happy and free from suffering. We may use it as a closing for our meditation sessions.

Coda

May all beings, with each of whom I am
profoundly connected,
Be happy and obtain the causes and
conditions of happiness.
May all beings, each of whom has been my most
*precious mother, countless number of times,**
Be free from suffering and the causes and
conditions of suffering.
May all beings be filled with unbridled
empathetic joy and
May all beings relate to friends and enemies
alike with equanimity and impartiality.
May I attain a measure of enlightenment
so that I may point others to the
Great happiness—the awakened mind of
compassion.
May I receive the blessings of this meditation
practice so that
Love and compassion, joy and equanimity,
Devotion and faith, and the power to help
May grow and flourish in my heart, naturally,
And that I may be free from
delusion and doubt.

* (Alternate phrase for reincarnation agnostics:)
May all beings, each of whom is a reflection
of my most precious loved one,

Meditation Session Five

Bring to mind an object towards which you feel devotion or gratitude. Focus on a concept, a symbolic image, a spiritual icon, or a pithy sentence until an associated feeling arises in your heart. Then let go of the object itself and allow the feeling of gratitude or devotion to unfold as you lose yourself in the nurturance of the process.

PART TWO

THE APPROACH

Chapter Four

Meditative Mindfulness

In the fifth century BCE, at dawn in Bodhgaya as the third watch was ending, a man named Siddhartha Gautama attained full enlightenment. His first words upon awakening as a Buddha were heard thusly:

The nectar-like truth is revealed,
Profound, serene, unfabricated,
Luminous, timeless, self-secret,
Non-conceptual, unconditioned.

These words point to the fruition of the process of becoming enlightened. While dwelling on Vulture Peak Mountain, the Buddha taught the primary qualities that awaken one to true enlightenment: the impartial attitude towards all beings; the altruistic frame of mind; the attitude of non-aggression; and the open mind that is receptive and holds no prejudice. The facts of our existential situation are that we are hardly awake nor are our minds normally quiet. To attain meditative serenity, the mind must be radically tamed by undertaking diligent training. Beginning with mindfulness practice as method and subsequently conjoining it with insight meditation practice allows innate wisdom to unfold.

Meditative mindfulness (Skt., *shamatha*) is the practice of the fifth paramita, mindfulness, of the Buddha's basic qualities or great perfections teaching.

Mindfulness arises as the result of continuous attentiveness to an object of meditation until the mind stabilizes naturally. Shamatha practice is a dualistic fixation on an object by a subject and is not contingent upon understanding the object's reality nor its status. Our state of meditative concentration becomes shamatha when our body and mind become pliable and at ease and rest in serenity. The full attainment of shamatha is characterized by the integrated feeling of well being, clarity, and non-thought.

Mindfulness or meditative serenity is not a trance nor is it being spaced-out. It is not an induced dull state of mind; it is an alert and undisturbed state of mind. It is not a mood of laxity and cannot be brought on by the use of alcohol, tobacco, drugs, sex, or the euphoria of success. Mindfulness practice conditions our mind to receive wisdom, the sixth paramita, and is like the preparation of a tea service: the cup must first be clean and empty, and then paired to a fine saucer with napkin and spoon. It must be receptive but not too eager, anticipative yet unexcited—entirely ready for service. Gathering the service ensemble is like the meditation practice; the experience of the tea is the meditation.

Attaining enlightenment, is primarily a matter of eliminating obstacles such as greed, anger, and ignorance. This works because, hidden beneath these afflictions, all of us are already a Buddha in disguise. To realize our potential buddhahood, the skins of illusion must be shed. Buddhist mindfulness practice is an integral part of this process. If our coffee cup is soiled, there is no need to toss it in the trash or buy a new one, simply wash it to remove the dirt and stains. This works because the cup itself is inherently clean, the dirt and stains are temporary add-ons.

Buddhist meditation practice undeniably produces secondary benefits such as relaxation skills, calmness, improved relationships, and refreshing sleep. On the other hand, many in-vogue mindfulness systems run counter to enlightenment because of their motivation to focus on self interests. Athletes use mindfulness techniques to enhance their performance. CEOs and hedge fund managers take mindfulness training sabbaticals to inflate their already excessive bank accounts. These are certainly beneficial in a materialistic sense but they only enhance ego clinging. For some, it may be more beneficial to take a day off and visit the beach, get a massage, have coffee with a friend, or enjoy a hot sauna.

Results of our actions depend on our goal and motivation. Right motivation is the altruistic aspiration for liberation from delusion, both for ourselves and others. The heart of the Buddha's teaching, the result of his insight, is the *dharma of bodhicitta.* In this context, the Sanskrit word "dharma" means both truth and duty. The Sanskrit word "bodhicitta" refers to the awakened mind of compassion. Thus, the dharma of bodhicitta is seeing the truth of the necessity for altruism in a world where all beings and actions are interconnected.

By closely observing the operation of the mind, we may notice thoughts and emotions flitting around like birds trapped in a closed room. If we practiced the breathing exercise in "Meditation Session Three" and tried to extend it for a few minutes, we may have become distracted by a profusion of thoughts and feelings. Nevertheless, noticing these distractions and returning to observing the breath is a sign of success and progress in our practice. All distractions may be viewed as friends of the practice.

The predominant habit pattern of our mind is becoming entangled with incessantly arising thoughts and emotions, which breed further cycles of confusion. Results of this entanglement range from the gross, explosive anger or terror, to the subtle, background discursiveness or dullness. Somewhere in between these are: desire, attachment, ambition, anxiety, worry, hubris, bigotry, and ignorance. Meditation is seeing into this disorder. To approach a meditative state, our mind must be quiet and reflective, like the limpid pool of a mountain lake, neither muddy below nor ripples above.

Enjoying the state of calm abiding is one of the skillful means for reflecting reality and attaining wisdom. Prompted by the right motivation, serenity is attained through steady and moderate mindfulness practice. There was a young mother who was intrigued by a meditation practice she found in a "spiritual" book. She became determined to sit in a difficult yoga posture for thirty minutes concentrating on religious verses. So she diligently practiced every morning with furrowed brow. One day, after a few weeks of practice, she was in the kitchen anxiously preparing lunch. Her five-year-old daughter was playing nearby, when seemingly out of the blue, she looked up and asked,

"Mommy, why is it that the more you meditate, the meaner you get?"

Ambitiously trying to force a noisy mind into the cage of meditation practice yields bitter fruit and is a sign of wrong motives. Meditation is about relaxing into awareness and allowing kindness and compassion to unfold naturally. Have patience, for we have long lived under the control of delusive mental habits.

This story of an obsessive concentration practice illustrates a common side-effect that causes internal tensions and may escalate into malicious behavior. We may experience an onslaught of repressed memories that cause us distress. If the feelings are too disturbing, we may consult with an experienced meditation teacher or psychotherapist. However, there is no danger associated with meditation practices that apply a common sense approach and employ mindfulness as a guardian.

The Meditator

One evening, in the little meadow of periwinkles beyond the fence surrounding my house, the blessed cat, with mindfulness and stealth, crept closer and closer to a poorly disguised gopher hole. He sat very still, all senses alert, concentrating with intense interest on the hole's entrance, or rather exit, from his perspective. Several distractions occurred but none were successful in diverting his attention. Obviously, he fully intended to draw that life within the hole into union with his life. Though he remained in a state of unruffled concentration, serenity was not present, nor was insight.

This tale is not to illustrate the meditation practice of a cat, but to highlight the fact that the ability to concentrate is quite common among predators and others. Witness the skill exhibited by all-star athletes, military sharpshooters, teen texters, and video gamers. Concentration alone is not sufficient to attain the wisdom of insight but is a necessary step towards enlightenment. The cat may capture the gopher, but is not yet awakened to empathy with the gopher's desire for life. For this insight to take root, motivation beyond mere attraction must govern the choice of object for meditation practice. The shamatha practice for meditative serenity forms the basis for the experience of compassion to arise through insight or vipashyana practice.

Meditation practice benefits from consideration of the preconditions embodied in the first four paramitas: generosity, discipline, patience, and enthusiasm. Being mindful of accomplishing these preconditions, we may select an appropriate object for practice according to our personality. For example, if our behavior is dominated by hatred, meditate on love. If discursiveness is dominant, focus on the breath. To understand the illusory nature of the self, reflect on the aggregates, the constituent elements of body and mind. (These will be detailed under "Composition of Self" in Chapter Nine). To deal with the causes of suffering, look at the mental afflictions. Nondiscursive objects such as the breath or a candle flame are useful for shamatha practice. Discursive objects such as love involve analytical thinking and are better reserved for vipashyana practice.

Take care in selecting the meditation practice object. Once there was a simple monk who wished to become a shamatha practitioner. After receiving some instructions from his teacher, he sat down in the temple, chose a cow as his meditation object, and began to diligently meditate on it. After many practice sessions, he went outside into a lush meadow, got down on all fours, and began eating the grass. Upon seeing all this, his teacher asked him why he was eating as a cow eats. With grass and weeds dangling from his mouth, the monk raised his head and replied: "Moo-ooo." Perhaps the cow-monk hadn't understood the purpose of meditation practice and became attached to the wrong meditative object.

Four Foundations of Mindfulness

When the Buddha began his teaching on meditation, he emphasized the application of mindfulness in one's daily activities. He formalized this practice in his famous discourse on mental training, *the Four Foundations of Mindfulness,* in which he described four categories of mental cultivation. These four forms of mindfulness meditation practice take as their objects: the body, the feelings, the mind, and the mental formations.

1. The first category of mental training is in connection with our body. We observe the breathing process, body postures, and physical sensations. This practice can be done in any situation by giving constant attention to our physical and verbal activities. An example of this is the practice of "walking meditation", wherein we carefully monitor the movement of our principal body parts while walking in a slow and deliberate manner. Another common practice while sitting is the moment to moment scanning of each body part, from the top of the head to the tip of each toe and becoming aware of its particular sensation. These practices entail being attentive and simply living in the present moment with full mindfulness.

2. The second category of mental cultivation regards our feelings. The practice is to be aware of whether our feelings are pleasant, unpleasant, or indifferent. When a feeling presents itself, examine its nature, how it arises and disappears in our mind, where

it comes from and where it goes, and whether or not we feel attached to it.

3. The third category of training is the meditation practice dealing with our mind itself. We may observe and be aware of the state of our mind both while it is at rest and in movement. We may be aware of whether our mind is with or without the afflictions of anger or resentment, excessive desire or attachment, and ignorance or stupidity. We may know whether it is distracted or not, attentive or not, and free or not.

4. The fourth category of mental cultivation is the mindfulness meditation practice using our own mental formations as objects. Mental formations are born from our psychological conditioning and take the form of subconscious habit patterns. To become accustomed to "seeing" thoughts and emotions arise, we may calmly notice these mental activities as they display themselves. Bare perceptions such as simply seeing birds playing or hearing the wind in the trees are not thoughts in this context. Our mind usually reacts to perceptions by generating mental formations such as concepts, labels, likes, dislikes, and indifferences drawn from our personal memory bank. Emotions are the energetic aspect of thoughts that get caught up in the ensuing drama.

In our meditation practice, we may observe, analyze, and reflect upon these mental objects. They include five principal obstacles to enlightenment: obsessive pursuit of pleasure, malice or ill will, laxity, anxiety, and uncertainty or distrust. They also include beneficial factors in support of the way to enlightenment such as: mindfulness, interest in sacred doctrines, energy, joy, relaxation, concentration, and equanimity. Traditionally, fifty two mental objects were delineated by the Buddha.

In the training for attaining the serenity of mindfulness, we may notice that mental states or levels of attention develop in discernible stages: initially focusing on an object, gradually eliminating distractions, and subsequently pacifying the mind until we dwell in equanimity. Through the practice of mindfulness, these beneficial mental states arise through our cultivation of virtue, especially enthusiastic diligence, until a state of calm abiding is experienced. Consequently, our awareness becomes alive: ever-present, spontaneous, effortless, and natural.

Meditation Session Six

Think about your personal predispositions and mental habit patterns and choose a useful meditative object for this mindfulness practice. Shamatha practice is more beneficial when using an object that is both meaningful and concise. When choosing a pithy sentence or paragraph, condense it to a single word or concept and allow it to arise. For example, if you are predisposed to viewing others as enemies, you may select the following passage from Rumi. Represent it by the word "love."

Whether you love the One
or another human being,
If you love enough,
in the end you will come into the
Presence of Love itself,

Stabilize your mind on *love* as the object with no accompanying analysis. Your focus on *love* will be like a feeling—a warmth, not as an imaged group of letters. Lose yourself while communing with the object such that there is no subject/object dualistic operation. This is not to identify yourself with the object but to lose yourself in its ambiance. Let go of any sense of effort and rest in calm abiding.

Meditation matures as one begins to shift focus from an object of awareness to the openness of awareness itself, like gazing into the vast sky rather than watching cloud formations.

Chapter Five

Meditative Insight

The contemporary Tibetan Buddhist meditation master, Chokyi Nyima Rinpoche, makes the point that: "One of our main tasks as human beings is to seek and to discover what is real and true. We must use intelligence as our main tool and sound reason as the verifier. That is all we have at this point. However, as we go about deepening our understanding, we still carry one problem with us: this mind that reasons so intelligently is still basically confused. Therefore, every 'insight' is saturated by confusion. … It is not unmistaken wisdom, and it is not authentic until complete enlightenment."

Shakyamuni Buddha, the sage of the Shakya clan, began his quest for the truth by following the ancient yogic practice of mindfulness meditation until he attained the highest sublime states of samadhi. However, he perceived that course of action to be insufficient for full enlightenment. Although he experienced relative peace for himself, it did not bring happiness and freedom from suffering to other beings. Seeing the need for something more, he initiated the practice of insight meditation (Skt., *vipashyana or* Pali, *Vipassana*). The essence of vipashyana practice is using attention and observation to transform mindfulness into full awareness of reality. Meditative insight unfolds as wisdom, the sixth paramita of the Buddha's basic qualities or great perfections teachings. Wisdom manifests as kindness and compassion with the capacity to alleviate the suffering of others.

The insight we are inquiring into is related to but not the same as intuition. The word "intuition" is defined in *the New Oxford American Dictionary* as "the ability to understand something immediately, without the need for conscious reasoning. [Intuition is] a thing that one knows or considers likely from instinctive feeling rather than conscious reasoning." Intuition may arise from various sources; for example, as a product of subconscious conditioning factors, paranoid thinking, and perhaps even paranormal perceptions. Witness the situation when an unresolved issue or a particularly vexing problem is carried into your cycle of sleeping and dreaming. If the solution magically appears upon awakening, the process of resolution may be attributed to the action of the subliminal continuity of thought and is called intuition. Insight, on the other hand, is based on a fully conscious examination and analysis of phenomena in order to see the true nature of things. Helena the Theosophist teaches that insight arises from practicing ". . . a clean life, an open mind, and a pure heart."

Intuition, as well as ordinary thinking, is conditioned by our total collective past—individual and cultural. A mind conditioned by fear and anger results in confusion and conflict. A free and open mind brings peace and insight. The yield from meditative insight resonates with the radical teaching of Jesus to *Resist not evil* and the Taoist teaching of *wu wei*, the effortless spontaneous alignment with right action.

The purpose of practicing vipashyana is to attain insight into the three marks of existence: impermanence, suffering, and non-self. The method of vipashyana practice is to look into the essence and nature of the mind. The ultimate goal is to know the reality of nonduality—to attain the view that sees the real nature of phenomena.

As we shall see in Chapter Six, "Union of Mindfulness and Insight", shamatha practice has prepared our mind to accommodate the process of vipashyana. Meditative insight conjoined with mindfulness breaks down our entrenched illusions and leads to the direct experience of reality

Four Noble Truths

Subsequent to his enlightenment, the Buddha journeyed to the Deer Park in Benares, India, where he chanced upon his former comrades—his ascetic fellow seekers. They were now ripe and receptive with "ears to hear," so he began the first "turning of the wheel of dharma" by giving a set of basic teachings that mirrored his insight into the nature of suffering. Known as the *Four Noble Truths*, they comprise teachings on the truth of suffering, the origin of suffering, the cessation of suffering, and the path of liberation from suffering.

1. Truth of suffering - Suffering is a fact of life; it is our primary existential condition. All sentient beings universally experience the burden of dissatisfaction. Generally, there are three kinds of suffering. First, the "suffering of suffering" is easily seen because it refers to the tangible pains associated with sickness and injury, hunger and thirst, fear, depression, and anxiety. Because of their limited mental capacity, animals and other creatures only seem to experience this type of suffering.

The second kind is the "suffering of change," which includes feelings of decline, disappointment, and boredom. We may notice that all pleasant feelings are temporary and often become precursors to misery or loss. For example, love for another, joyful at first, waxes and wanes. Our love may take the form of possessiveness. Jealousy may displace love if the other's affections turn to someone else. The object of our love may grow mean or ugly, so our love may turn into indifference or hatred. In any case, love becomes grief when the loved one dies. In his poem "Keramos", Henry Wadsworth Longfellow speaks of this impermanence.

Turn, turn my wheel!
All things must change to something new,
to something strange.
Nothing that is can pause or stay;
The moon will wax, the moon will wane,
The mist and cloud will turn to rain,
The rain to mist and cloud again,
Tomorrow be to-day.

The third kind of suffering is the anxiety of uncertainty: sensing a hidden danger, feeling that all is not well, that something is not quite right—incomplete—unfinished. Ever-present, it manifests as a fundamental discontent, an indeterminate feeling that there is more to life than eating and defecating, working and taking pleasure, or sleeping like a corpse.

Because there is me, the separate self, there is mine. If my mother is sad, I feel sad. If my child is bullied at school, I feel her pain. Even if I am not aware of specifics, I know that all my loved ones eventually experience suffering. If my car is scratched, I suffer disappointment. If my wealth disappears, I experience the suffering of loss. In any event, I know that all my things are constantly deteriorating. Collectively, these adverse occurrences to my possessions generate a pervasive feeling of helplessness that is always present. This suffering is normally felt indirectly and may not be experienced at all if the objects belong to someone else. I don't feel heart broken if the Wall Street banker loses money or if a stranger's ball team loses the game. Nevertheless, there remains an underlying awareness of the immense sadness and suffering in the world. Consciously acknowledging this awareness quickens the gestation of our dormant seeds of compassion.

This third type of suffering is not a tangible experience of misery or unhappiness but rather a subtle sense of being conditioned or limited, like a prisoner in a low security "white collar" jail. We may feel inauthentic or lost, like a fish when transferred from its ocean home to a small tank. Perhaps we sense the double-pronged existential angst of uncertainty and inevitability, the indeterminate outcome of our self-becoming process in tandem with our subconscious certainty and fear of the fact that we will die.

2. The truth of the origin of suffering - The Buddha taught that all suffering stems from the root causes introduced in Chapter Two, "Preparing the Garden of Meditation". These are the three afflictions of excessive desire, hatred, and ignorance—also called the three poisons of attachment, aggression, and delusion. These causes manifest as all-pervasive suffering in the dungeon of our defiled mental states. Suffering has been perpetuated since beginningless time through the actions of karma, both individual and collective. The seeds of karma gathered from this life as well as from past lives are stored in our personal

memory bank. When conditions are right, they sprout and grow: manifesting as happiness or unhappiness in this and succeeding lives.

These root causes come from an even more basic cause—ego cherishing or self-centeredness. Arising from mistaken self identity and the lack of awareness of the illusory nature of phenomena, samsara, the cycle of suffering, is established and continues until enlightenment is attained. The momentary bliss of *egonorance*, the ignorance of holding the notion of being a separate self entity, is merely a temporary and illusory happiness. This concept will be discussed in Chapter Nine, "Origin of the Self".

3. The truth of cessation of suffering - Although suffering knows no boundaries, it can be ended. There is a way out of the darkness of chaos and into the light of liberation for all beings. That is the purpose of our journey of awakening and radical transformation.

4. The truth of the path of liberation - The basic dharma teachings of the Buddha lead to the liberation from suffering for those who strive to be free. For forty five years, he primarily taught the way of the Noble Eightfold Path grouped under eight aspects: right view, right intention, right speech, right action, right livelihood, right effort, right mindfulness, and right meditation. Briefly summarized, these guidelines are:

1. Right view is recognizing the truth of non-duality, that there is no independently existing self. It

understands the Four Noble Truths and how reality and suffering are linked.

2. Right intention is holding the motivation to liberate all beings from suffering and to renounce our selfish desire, malice, and violence.

3. Right speech is to refrain from harming another through slander, malicious words, and gossip.

4. Right action is to do no harm and do good to others. It is moral conduct that refrains from killing, stealing, lying, and sexual misconduct.

5. Right livelihood is making a living that brings no harm to others. Harmful professions include trading in weapons or alcohol, cheating, killing animals, etc.

6. Right effort is to avoid evil states of mind and to foster wholesome states of mind.

7. Right mindfulness is the practice of shamatha which entails being aware of the activities of the body, feelings, mind states, and thought formations.

8. Right meditation is the skillful practice of vipashyana or insight meditation to benefit all beings.

The Buddha "turned the wheel of dharma" a second time and generated a subsequent set of teachings that emphasize the wisdom of compassion. Real happiness for all beings comes when selfishness has been transformed into altruism. Vipashyana or insight meditation practice is primarily associated with the first aspect, right view, and the eighth aspect, right meditation. It takes the very nature of mind itself as its object.

Four Reminders

The Buddha taught a particular set of considerations or thoughts to turn the mind to aid us on this path. The *Four Reminders*, sometimes called the *Four Mind Changings*, are observable facts regarding everyone's present status of being. They include the preciousness of this human life, the verity of impermanence and death, the actions of karma, and the defects of samsara. Although we may understand these important facts intellectually, they may not be sufficiently ingrained in our consciousness to affect our way of living. Reflecting on these ideas can change the way we view the world.

1. Preciousness of this human life: Recognizing the preciousness of this human body causes us to realize and appreciate our relatively fortunate situation of having the capacity to follow a spiritual path. This realization may encourage a deeper inquiry into the meaning of this particular life. Ponder the infinite possibilities. What are the numerical odds of our being born in a human body versus a pig or a fish or even a microbe? On obtaining a human body, what are the odds of being born in a country free of war and famine? How likely are we to find a friendly neighborhood, a nurturing family, a healthy body and mind, freedom from poverty, opportunity for education, and the leisure to pursue spiritual matters? So – O' Pilgrims, are we not amongst the fortunate?

2. Impermanence and death: Recognizing the truth of impermanence, the precariousness of favorable situations, the fragility of loving relationships, and the certainty that death is one breath away may spur us to undertake meaningful actions without procrastination. Living things decay and return to dust; mountains erode and become deserts; even diamonds may be crushed into dust. Our faith in government operations at all levels declines. The climate is rapidly changing and becoming harsher and more unpredictable. Wages that once increased every year now lose value. The car needs repair and a treasured coat is threadbare. Mundane tasks such as washing dishes, grooming hair, and cleaning waste must be endlessly repeated and are never finished. Enthusiasm for a favorite pastime grows dull and old joys fade like spent flowers. Our former soul mate now loves another. Aging is relentless and death is inevitable.

3. Action of karma - Karma is the universal law of cause and effect. It is perfect justice that for every effect, there must have been a cause. Karma is like gravity, its action is certain, unfathomable, and impersonal regardless of which planet you stand on. If we sow apple seeds, we will grow apple trees and harvest apples. If we drink poison, we will get sick and may die. If we are kind and generous, we will be loved. These simple examples of karma in action echo the biblical verse:

for whatsoever a man soweth,
that shall he also reap

However, unlike gravity, the manifestations of karma are not generally predictable. Karma is not preordained fate, although it sometimes seems to be a reward or punishment for specific deeds. The actions of karma are extremely subtle and complex because the relationship between cause and effect depends on a multitude of unknown factors. The way in which karma manifests is further mystifying because we do not remember our past lives plus the fact that we change every moment and are not quite the same person that we were a few years ago. One of the most pertinent conditions—the motivation of the doer is especially difficult to ascertain.

The concepts of karma and reincarnation form a beautiful synthesis for understanding why bad things happen to good people. Causes born of the actions of this and previous lives are stored as karmic seeds in our personal memory bank and are certain to play out. When the right conditions and circumstances arise, the beneficial seeds s may be watered and nourished by love and compassion and the bad seeds may be burned in the fires of meditation and a pure life. Recognizing the inevitable consequences of karma naturally causes us to be more mindful of the actions of our body, speech, and mind. We may even feel prompted to obey the biblical injunction:

do unto others
as you would have them
do unto you.

For those who do not believe that karma and reincarnation are facts, the idea of justice and fair play becomes a logical conundrum. For those who believe in the Abrahamic God and think that some of the suffering in this world is unjust or immoral, His benevolence can only be described as an unfathomable enigma.

4. Defects of samsara - Reflecting on this fourth reminder—the pervasiveness of suffering, the perpetual dissatisfaction with or incompleteness of life leads to a relaxation of everyday anxieties and worries. Attachment to hopes and fears begins to loosen and disentangle. Thus may our mind and heart open to new directions for spiritual growth.

Insight Practice

The Himalayan Buddhist tradition primarily practiced in Tibet, Nepal, and Bhutan is based on the Buddha's "second turning of the wheel of dharma". It includes and goes beyond the Buddha's initial teachings on mindfulness and liberation. The practice of insight meditation or vipashyana, in this tradition, is concerned with gaining insight into the ultimate non-dual nature of reality—the union of cognizance and emptiness (Skt., *shunyata*). In the end stages of vipashyana, the subtle presence of a meditator is absent, yet the nature of mind is experienced. To reiterate, there is an initial level or stage of meditative insight that looks at phenomena including ideas or concepts, and a subsequent stage actively concerned with the nature of that which is looking—mind itself.

The Dalai Lama points out a subtle distinction in the objects of meditation. Concepts such as love, emptiness, or selflessness may be selected as objects for shamatha practice. For example, assume that the idea of love is selected as the object. One reflects on its meaning and then one apprehends it. In sharp contrast, one may focus on love's absolute aspect from the perspective of vipashyana practice. This meditation on love wouldn't mean taking love as an object, but rather "seeking to transform our whole state of mind into that state of love or compassion."

As described in Chapter Six, "Union of Mindfulness and Insight", shamatha is merged with vipashyana to look into the nature of the body and mind, their constituent elements, and their ultimate lack of inherent existence. These reflections are prerequisites for approaching the reality of non-duality in which there is no subject/object dichotomy.

Meditation Session Seven

Select a profound idea or concept with the goal of increasing your understanding of it. Analyze its meaning in detail while concentrating one-pointedly on the meditation object. After reflecting in this manner, drop the focusing and allow a non-discursive relationship to unfold. Rest in the ambience of the process.

Chapter Six

Union of Mindfulness and Insight

When approaching meditation practice, it is necessary to have both a purposeful aim and right effort. The aim is simply to awaken from our dream-like world to reality. The method is to connect the practices of shamatha and vipashyana meditation. The Dalai Lama teaches that if one doesn't explore the analytic faculty of the mind through the practice of vipashyana and merely remains absorbed in the serenity of shamatha—simply resting in the bliss of nonconceptuality, then intelligence becomes dull and the wisdom to discriminate between right and wrong is impaired.

It is insufficient to cultivate either serenity or insight alone to travel the path to enlightenment. Tradition gives the example of using an oil lamp to view a picture in the middle of the night. If the lamp is both bright and undisturbed by the wind, the details of the picture will be very clear and sharp. Otherwise, if the lamp is dim or is bright but flickering in the wind, the image details will be dull. Similarly, to clearly understand the profound meaning, we need the brightness of the vipashyana that discerns the meaning of reality, as well as the stability and unwavering attention of shamatha. The Dalai Lama teaches that possessing an intellectual understanding of reality is not sufficient to fully understand the reality of things because one will be "disturbed by the winds of uncontrollably fluctuating discursive thought."

Calm abiding is necessary to establish the basis for authentic insight to arise, but this shamatha practice alone does not result in enlightenment. Shamatha practice begins with a meditator and an object of meditation. Ironically, it is this dualistic fixation that obscures pristine awareness; hence the need for the union of shamatha and vipashyana. In the end stages of meditation practice, the meditation object becomes awareness itself and the meditator/object dichotomy dissolves into the meditation of non-meditation.

Mindfulness temporarily suppresses afflictions such as anger, greed, and ignorance; however, it is the light of insight that eradicates their seeds. Wisdom is the result of an integrative process that occurs spontaneously with the union of serenity and insight. From the analytical meditation of vipashyana, true knowledge of reality arises while the meditation of shamatha sustains and stabilizes it. Weaving the warp and weft of shamatha and vipashyana into the fabric of wholeness is the necessary action for attaining enlightenment. When this union has been attained, compassion naturally arises as the capacity for relieving the suffering of ourselves and others.

To skillfully traverse this path, we must have a warrior like alertness with sharp discrimination. Signs begin to arise during our journey that indicate the proximity of an ever present dangerous obstacle—the abyss of self-cherishing. This abyss has the power to draw us deeper into samsara—the whirlpool of cyclic existence. Therein it can swallow our spiritual aspirations and intentions. In preparing for this stage of our journey, we focused on meditation objects that address general impediments. To confront this most formidable obstacle of self-cherishing, the union of shamatha and vipashyana initiates the process of reorienting our view towards selflessness as the meditation object. The abyss is there and must be crossed to continue the journey up the mountain path of meditative inquiry. The view of selflessness will be examined in Chapter Nine, "Origin of the Self".

Meditative serenity has the characteristics of: nondiscursiveness, unwavering attention on a single object, clarity that is free from laxity and excitement, and the benefit of joyfulness. The mark of serenity is that attention stays where it is placed without distraction. One of the greatest marks of insight is to know the reality of selflessness. The great Indian sage Asanga says: "Because the path of serenity is unencumbered by striving, insight is pure, clean, comes after serenity, and is fully suffused with delight. Therefore, your serenity and insight combine and are balanced; this is called the path of the union of serenity and insight."

Meditation Session Eight

As your mind and body become quiet and relaxed, notice thoughts or emotions as they arise. Without becoming enamored with their content nor getting entangled with them, just let them go their own way. Reflect on the process of thoughts arising and disappearing. Where did they come from? Where do they abide? Where do they go? Allowing this inquiry to fade away, rest attentively.

PART THREE

INTEGRATION

The Valley

Chapter Seven

Meditation and Beauty

The cultivation of meditation is like leaves on a tree readying themselves for the approach of winter. They draw and process nutrients from the soil in preparation for their role in sustaining the life of the tree. After a period of quietude, the leaves wither and fall to the earth; their task for this cycle is complete.

In meditation, as in death, there is beauty in the dissolving of delusion into the ground of being wherein pristine awareness is nurtured and renewed. During our climb on this mountain of inquiry, we may have seen that the real meaning of meditation is beyond concepts. Perhaps we cannot really know what meditation is, but we may know what it is not.

Experience of Beauty

Occasionally, we have the good fortune of coming upon a phenomenon of breathtaking beauty. An experience arises that is full of splendor and bliss, defying description. However, the fidelity of its memory soon degrades and we realize the memory is not the beauty.

A panoramic view of the immense valley suddenly revealed itself.
Across the glowing green fields, the glorious sunset

spread its wings over the mountaintops.
At the instant of perception,
just before the formation of conceptions
Bliss enveloped the whole earth!

Prior to the onset of mundane pleasure,
Intense joy and an ineffable sense of timelessness
and sheer beauty arose.
In that initial contact, there was no subject looking
and no object of looking;
There was only pure awareness, naked—unadulterated.
Beauty was complete and alone!
Time itself was not.

Assertively, without apology, the response of pleasure
and its acquisitive tendencies suddenly engulfed my
experience and intruded upon the pure perception.
The fullness of the original beauty went into hiding,
never again to expose itself.
What happened to the beauty?

Conditioned habit patterns sprang into action with
cunning abruptness.
My mind sought to reify the extraordinary experience,
to enlarge itself.
I named, measured, captured, possessed, and struggled
to sustain the experience.
Thought, in pursuit of becoming, once again consumed
the moment, thus increasing its storehouse of
self-referential experience.

The desire for security and continuity correlates

with the response of grasping,
Which leads to self-embalming—preserving that which is already dead.

Can the pristine be seen through the veil of conditioning?
Can the mind come upon beauty without destroying it?

Helena the Theosophist's "Voice of the Silence", asks: *Is the mind the great slayer of the real?*

In the interval between the first contact of perception and the initiation of the thought process, love and beauty flourish. Similarly, where there is no selfishness, no motive, no desire for special experience, meditation freely sheds the accoutrements of conditioning and fully blossoms. From Mabel Collins' "Light on the Path":

> *In the deep silence the mysterious event will occur which will prove that the way has been found. Call it by what name you will, it is a voice that speaks where there is none to speak. It is a messenger that comes, a messenger without form or substance; or it is the flower of the soul that has opened. It cannot be described by any metaphor.*

When the personal ego is operative, meditation will not enter the sanctuary of the heart. Seeing the truth of this leads to the unfolding of the mystical power of love. Before one can experience this ineffable love, the *giant weed of self* must be burned in the flame of meditation. Again from "Light on the Path":

> *Grow as the flower grows, unconsciously, but eagerly anxious to open its soul to the air. So must you press forward to open your soul to the Eternal. But it must be the Eternal that draws forth your strength and beauty —not desire of growth for in the one case you develop in the luxuriance of purity; In the other you harden by the forcible passion for personal stature.*

Referring to meditation in "Freedom from the Known", Krishnamurti comments:

> *One asks oneself then whether it is possible to come upon this thing without inviting, without waiting, without seeking or exploring—just for it to happen like a cool breeze that comes in when you leave the window open. You cannot invite the wind but you must leave the window open.*

Meditation Session Nine

This session is to integrate the meditation practice into daily life and so will not be a formal "sitting" practice. Bring awareness to your specific current situation. While out walking, be aware of thoughts and emotions arising and dissolving. Notice the quality of your attention while changing a diaper, doing dishes, greeting a neighbor, or watching someone comb their hair. While driving a car, witness the fear or anger that arises when a stranger rudely blows their horn. What is the nature of the impatience felt during traffic delays? In summary, this practice is to simply be mindfully aware of thoughts and feelings as they occur. Do not judge, control, repress, manipulate, obsess, understand, or become attached to them. If you are fortunate, meditation may arise in the gap between your succession of thoughts.

Chapter Eight

Search for the Self

Cloud Formations

On an ordinary sunny day,
while lying in the company of the other
flowers and creatures of the meadow,
the child watched the clouds
form their fantasy shapes and figures
in the open sky above.
The vastness of the bright space
invited wonderment
and the question arose in his mind:
Who am I?

This generated a deluge of thoughts
which culminated in his pondering
the meaning of death.
Being familiar with the fact that
people and animals die,
does it follow that I die when my body dies?

So began a childhood quest to understand the relationship between the "I" and the body. To approach this problem in a rigorous scientific manner, he employed a thought experiment using his unbound imagination. He mentally removed his body parts one by one, starting with his toes and finishing with the top of his head. Each part was checked to see if any part of his self was hidden in it. As each part was eliminated, the residue was systematically examined to see if a sense of "I" was there. After hypothetically removing all body parts in this manner, he happily concluded that "I" was indeed still present—in fact, quite near. He began to think: *I am not really my body.* His sense of self seemed to exist as a nebulous center in the space encompassing the general locale of his head and heart. Through this line of inquiry, he began to see that identification with his body was a mistaken view and that *body* is merely a concept, a name assigned to a collection of body parts. After his experience of dissociation from the body, no overt fear of death or loss was felt since a feeling of "I" always seemed to remain. An intimation of immortality lingered; yes, completely losing oneself was simply unimaginable. Although from the force of habit, he still tended to identify with his body; these particular bonds of illusion were forever weakened. The first step towards liberation had occurred.

Beyond leading to the recognition of not being the body, the "removing parts" analysis changed the very basis for belief in the existence of "I" from *my* body to *a* mind. A new primary factor of self-identification began to focus on the mind with its thoughts and feelings. After all, where there are thoughts and feelings, there must be a thinker and feeler; thus the child became an unwitting fellow traveler with Descartes and his baggage: "I think, therefore, I am." The conclusion of this phase of analysis seems to be that: *I am a mind and I have a body.*

However, a new conundrum arose when the child noticed the habitual tendency to make reference to *my* mind: *my* mind went blank; *my* mind is confused; I am out of *my* mind, etc. This conundrum may also be conflicted with thoughts about a soul: I hope *my* soul will be saved from hell; *my* soul will rest in the hereafter, etc. In this context, the terms "mind" and "soul" are essentially synonymous. In either case, there seems to be a different entity, a possessor self, separate from the mind or the soul. What is the nature of this entity who conceptualizes *mine*? Does it constitute the real self?

Unlike the body (including the brain and the nervous system), the mind is intangible. Nevertheless, the mind is made up of parts such as thoughts, perceptions, feelings, emotions, memories, and a variety of processed sense faculty imprints. Unfortunately, the "removing parts" analysis used to determine that the "I" was not the body is not so readily adaptable to the question: *Am I the mind?* Although I definitely experience and relate to these mental parts, they are clearly not me.

A different analytical approach will be applied to examine this issue and endeavor to look into the nature of the mind itself. The mind apprehends the body but cannot directly perceive itself. It can only think about or produce concepts depicting the mind. It can only infer its own existence. What is the referent for the mind?

Although it obviously functions, the mind itself appears to be an intangible accumulation of memories, thoughts, feelings, and experiences. Am I merely a reservoir of conditioned mental parts? By looking into each of these mental elements and systematically eliminating them as comprising the "I," the child reasonably concluded that identification with the mind was also a mistaken view. Although the imprint of the perennial habit of "I" was still present, it had faded a bit more. The next step towards liberation had irreversibly occurred.

The Nominal Self

Returning to the status of the child's understanding: from merciful ignorance, the thought lingered that *because thinking was present, surely I really existed.* That reasoned conception camouflaged itself behind a mask of self-assurance and a comfortable feeling of security. That feeling would have been short-lived if the child looked under the bed into the face of the ghostly omen, the death mask of the beloved "I"—the perennial semantic fiction.

Let us try a direct, down-to-earth, personal experiential approach to the question of the "I". Sit in a quiet place and ask: *Who am I?* The initial set of answers might go: *I am Mary; I am a person who wishes to be rich; I am the parent of my children; I am afraid of losing my loved one; I am the owner of that thing; I am jealous; I love flowers; I was a beauty queen; I will become president someday, ad infinitum.* All these responses relate to a self-image derived from past memories or future projections. They also indicate that the sense of self, *me* in contradistinction to *you* or *it*, is reinforced by identifying with our own desires, fears, and possessions. After all, it is logical to think that where there are possessions there must be a possessor.

Let us repeat our inquiry with an additional constraint: Imagine a sudden case of amnesia wherein all psychological and individual memories are erased. The only thought remaining is the present question: *Who am I?* You might think: *I'm sitting on a chair in a quiet room; I see furniture and an open window; I smell roses; my back aches; my eyelid itches; and I don't know who I am.*

These thoughts don't derive from a previous self-image but are the direct immediate perception associated with experiencing these sensory stimuli; there is still a bodily referent and a sense of possession. Thought has created an "I" that owns its response to stimuli: my place, my visions, my pain, and my anxiety. Thus the process of building a self-image began by identifying with the thoughts or feelings arising within.

Again, let us add another constraint and probe even deeper into the presumed existence of the "I". Imagine being in an isolation chamber with no external sensory inputs and a completely anesthetized body. This setup is more sophisticated and radical than the child's initial thought experiment of eliminating body parts. Again, assume that memories are wiped completely clean except for the initial question: *Who am I?* Under these conditions would I know *who* I am? I can't know *where* I am or *what* I am doing because there are no sensory inputs. There is no dreaming because there is no past to remember and no future to ponder, for the future is based on projections from the past. Would thoughts arise under these conditions? Internally, I may long for a reference point—a visceral centeredness—a living presence. At this stage, perhaps there remains only a pure unconditioned nondual awareness with no subject/object relationship.

The purpose of this foregoing process, the search for the self, was to find a logical basis for existence of a real self. Other than our nominal self, we have not been able to find a separate independent self. This begs the story of Benjamin Franklin when asked: "If we call a tail a leg, how many legs does a donkey have?" He answered: "Four. Calling a tail a leg doesn't make it one!"

We too have determined the existence of an "I" is merely imputed; the self is a name we assign to a collection of mental and physical parts;. Seeing the truth in this, we still act as if we are separate selves; however, we may notice that our relationships have mellowed, attachments and entanglements have relaxed, and the walls of demarcation with others have started to crumble. Perhaps there may be less violence. Signs of this deeper understanding occur when confusion, aggression, attachment, and the substratum of narcissism begin to dissipate and lose dominance over our life. The nineteenth century Irish philosopher Wei Wu Wei points out, "All our actions are essentially to benefit our self—and yet there isn't a self."

From the viewpoint of ultimate truth, there is no independently existent self. From the viewpoint of relative truth, a center of consciousness or ego appears and functions. In fact, we originally produced our own ego and continue to maintain it. Western psychology teaches that each human being experiences a process of self-development that ideally leads to a feeling of high self-esteem. So let us not disparage this self but relate to it as if it were a character in a movie or play. We may make friends with it, for it serves as a convenient referent. However, the habit of ego-identification or self-reification is the ultimate addiction and source of our suffering.

The Self and Dying

Having heard that when people die their souls continue on to heaven or hell or took rebirth in a new body, the child wondered: Am I a soul that possesses a mind and a body? Is this apparent conception of me—the soul, also delusional and impermanent like the body and mind—hence, no real existence? The discrimination of insight necessary to resolve these imponderables had not yet matured in his mind; nor had they been gifted to him by an outside power, so his quest was stymied.

If the child had carried the inquiry further, some subtle aspects of the self-nature may have revealed themselves: the innate desire for self-continuity; the instinctive self-referencing in all relationships; the constant striving to become more; and the undercurrent of existential angst from the fear of dying. Obviously the body dies and returns to dust. But does the soul or the self die? Modern research into near-death experiences suggest that our mind may not totally vanish into the great dustbin. It is often heard that you only live once; but it may be more accurate to think that you only live once *at a time.*

Most religious traditions believe in some type of afterlife. The Abrahamic religions assert that when we die, our soul withdraws from the physical body and moves to another realm permanently. There it either goes to heaven where it experiences communion with *God and Angels* or it goes to a fiery hell of eternal damnation supervised by the *Devil.* Some traditions add a purgatory or an in-between locale. The Abrahamic religions own the concept of *original sin*. Stemming from the disobedience by our first ancestors, the Creator endows all humans at birth with this *great existential burden*.

Western psychology does not acknowledge the role of reincarnation in the process of human development. They believe a sense of self begins to appear in early childhood and is primarily determined by genetics and environment. They give no consideration to the carryover karmic effects of past lives.

The more esoteric forms of the Abrahamic religions such as the Gnostic Christians, the Kabalistic Jews, and the Muslim Sufis hold the belief in reincarnation that, shortly after death, the mind or mental body transmigrates to a new physical body.

The Buddhists, as well as the Jains and many indigenous peoples, hold similar views but explicitly include the inseparability of karma and reincarnation in their conception. Governed by our personal karma, accumulated from this and previous lives, the cyclic process of rebirth continues until the attainment of liberation and enlightenment. Without the role of reincarnation, there is no mechanism in the operation of karma to balance the equation of causes and effects. There would not be enough time for karma to play out. What if a person robbed a bank, spent all the money on a life of pleasure, and suddenly died once and for all, could perfect justice be served?

In the Buddha's view, each person is born with a unique residue of unfinished good and bad karma accumulated from previous lives. This inheritance includes the habit of ego-identification. Perhaps it is this burden that resonates with the Abrahamic notion of *original sin*.

The cells of the physical body are constantly renewed, so the body as a whole also changes. Yet, every moment in our life stream seems to be a continuity wherein the self of the past meets the present, modifies or conditions itself, and projects itself into the future. Through habit we reify this continuity as a referent "I", even though this "I" of today is in fact different from the "I" of yesterday. When using the flame of a candle to light a second candle, the flame of the second to light a third, etc., it is not said that the flame of the first candle is the same as the flame of the third candle; nevertheless, they are dependently connected. Similar to the candle flame, when you die, the same you is not reborn. There may not be an immutable self; yet there is an apparent continuity.

Considering that living is the ongoing process of propagating the self through experience and memory, then dying may be defined as the ending of the self's identification with and attachment to "me" and "mine." What does it mean for an ordinary attachment to die. Once upon a time, I was heavily addicted to cigarettes. Each New Year, I would resolve to quit smoking and I did, temporarily. However, after a week or so, I began to take one cigarette after dinner as a reward for exercising my will power. The situation soon escalated back to a pack a day. This cycle was repeated for several years until the auspicious evening. I happened to be smoking while holding and rocking my baby daughter to sleep. She began to cough and I suddenly experienced an epiphany of revulsion to the act of smoking. My desire to smoke spontaneously and totally disappeared. The previous smoking self died a beautiful death there and then. A new self, free of the addictive attachment, was born in that rocking chair. This new self barely relates to the old self. The obsession of craving along with its anxiety completely vanished. Only a gray wisp of memory, an inauthentic artifact, remains. This particular process of dying was beyond motive, will, thought, and time.

What are the features of death when there are no attachments? Is it possible to die to all psychological afflictions? When we instinctively nurture a wounded bird, when we give unconditional kindness to another, when we do a truly unselfish act, our self is in suspension. In that moment, our self-center does not exist but nevertheless, there is joy. Every moment we die to the self we experience a new birth. Each time an old viewpoint or habit effortlessly drops because of the play of insight, there is a mental renewal, a rebirth. What then is the basis for the fear of dying? As sleep comes near and while we are still lucid, we may observe the onset of a kind of dying. There is no unfinished work, no unfulfilled expectations; all is complete; all is right, and that is the beauty of death. In the deep sleep beyond dreaming, our sense of self is in a state of suspended gestation. The mantle of the fear of death has dissolved like a blanket of frost in the rays of the sun.

Through seeing into the truth of emptiness, the fear of death withers at the root, for that which dies was never real in the first place.

Like a blind man who has once seen a flash of light,
one will never forget the experience of non-duality.
Nurture this glimpse of reality into flowering and
one's joyful aspiration is fulfilled.
Compassion for all beings,
wisdom in all things, and
genuine humility mark the fully enlightened.

Meditation Session Ten

Wherever you are, relax and be vividly aware of your environment: the sounds of the wind in the trees, birds singing, rain pattering on the roof, car traffic, children playing, and all other outer sounds within your compass. Also be aware of the inner sounds of the breath, throbbing of the pulse, and the subtle frequencies of the nervous system itself. Allow the outer and inner sounds to merge into a symphony of silence. The stage is set for the blessing of insight to come. Rest in that ambience.

Chapter Nine

Origin of the Self

Once upon a time, while working in the garden, a rather simple person received a sudden flashback to a moment of beginning. The strange feeling came not as a dream or conscious recall but a magical tuning-in to the indelible records of human memory. The first moment of becoming self-conscious was remembered; although this particular life entity already existed, there were no referent personal pronouns for its past existence. Using the vernacular of Helena the Theosophist, this day-dreamt story unfolds.

Origin of Me

In a beginning—but
In the middle of the third prototype phase,
On the fourth globe of this fourth round of the amalgamated cosmic dust of humanity,
The seed conception of "I" hovered somewhere above.
It had not yet found a fertile field for taking root.

While walking down the road to mythical Damascus,
The higher angels, with dubious benevolence, descended upon the innocent beast.
Suddenly there was me—myself in solitary movement.
Spontaneously and magically, possessions came into being: my hands, my feet, my body, my food, and my ax.

Dance with Samsara

Having accumulated little experience beyond mere survival instincts and
With only a functional sense of division from others,
Primordial innocence nevertheless tenuously remained.

However, as intelligence evolved, innate virtue began to dissipate.
Soon there was my wife, my family, my tribe, my country, and inevitably – my enemy.
New wombs pregnant with beings afflicted with the delusion of self-separateness began to appear.
Fated to be immersed in the murk of attachment and aversion, three kinds of sufferings arose.
Other beings began to participate in the collateral collusion to propagate this new entity, the Self.

This gestation environment supported and nourished the root of suffering—the belief in a real self—Me—in contradistinction to you.
This development, the biblical original sin, occurred long ago.

But wait up! Just this morning, I was walking down an unusually quiet road to Damascus,
When suddenly, with a burst of light, there was no I walking; there was only walking!
This anachronistic experience was short lived and I soon found myself back in the world of duality.

Had I traversed a magic bridge or
Had I only briefly glimpsed the other shore in a moment of luck or grace?

Must I, by my own self-conscious efforts, breach the wall
of selfishness and reenter the immaculate womb?
Was this an epiphany with demand for commitment?

Composition of Self

The Swiss author Hermann Hesse in his *Treatise on the Steppenwolf* says: "Man is an onion made up of a hundred integuments, a texture made up of many threads. The ancient Asiatics knew this well enough, and in the Buddhist Yoga an exact technique was devised for unmasking the illusion of the personality. The human merry-go-round sees many changes: The illusion that cost India the efforts of thousands of years to unmask is the same illusion that the West has labored just as hard to maintain and strengthen."

Ken Wilber, in his visionary book *The Eye of Spirit,* addresses the separate-self by observing that the realizations of the nondual traditions are uncompromising: there is only Spirit; there is only emptiness or spaciousness in all its radiant wonder. He says that the separate-self is ". . . at bottom, simply a sensation of seeking. When you feel yourself right now, you will basically feel a tiny interior tension or contraction—a sensation of grasping, desiring, wishing, wanting, avoiding, resisting—it is a sensation of effort."

The Buddha taught that all sentient beings are composed of five aggregates or sets of elements that comprehensively constitute the being's body-mind complex. These are generalized categories, loosely structured yet exhaustively inclusive of the totality of elements comprising a living being. The first group is material and the other four are mental. The Buddha illustrated this concept by pouring five heaps of rice on the ground, intermingling with each other at their edges, to show that the distinct elements of body and mind are intimately interconnected. The five aggregates are generally given as: form, feeling, perception, mental formations, and consciousness.

1. The aggregate of form refers to the materiality of things. It includes our physical body; the six sense organs: eyes, ears, nose, tongue, tactile receptors, and brain; and their corresponding six subjective sense registrations or impressions: seeing, hearing, smelling, tasting, touching, and thinking.

2. The aggregate of feeling comprises all of our physical, emotional, and mental responses to sensations. Predominately pain or pleasure, feelings are categorized under three types: pleasant, unpleasant, and neutral, depending on our preferences.

3. The aggregate of perception relates to the abstractions of qualities. Examples include: the color blue, a triangle, a circular shape, the taste of honey, the odor of roses, and stillness.

4. The aggregate of mental formations is the collective volitional activity of ideation and image or concept making. Examples include: compassion, love, hate, anger, attention, will, determination, confidence, concentration, ideals, moods, wisdom, ignorance, conceit, concept of self, attachment, and aversion. This aggregate is the unique generator of the actions of karma, the accumulation of causes and effects that accompany our life stream.

5. The aggregate of consciousness refers to the awareness of things—phenomena both physical and subtle. The Buddhist science of mind delineates eight

types of consciousnesses. The first five refer to the familiar senses of sight, sound, odor, taste, and touch.

The sixth or mental consciousness comprises the mind and its involvement with actions of thoughts and emotions. It functions as the process of thinking that directly uses information gleaned through the first five senses. This mentation is primarily conditioned by the seventh and eighth consciousnesses.

The seventh consciousness is the source of the feeling of a separate self, which is the primary cause of our unhappiness. This self-cherishing function overlays and permeates the entire spectrum of consciousness. It is called the afflictive consciousness because it is the root of the poisonous emotions of anger, hatred, jealousy, and envy.

The eighth consciousness, referred to as our storehouse consciousness, accesses our latent karma including memories and subconscious motives generated in this and previous lives. It is also characterized as the collective unconsciousness because it includes elements such as the potential for war, famine, and plague shared by others. This consciousness absorbs and is conditioned by cultural factors in our environment. Hence the importance of discrimination when faced with the choice of acquaintances, occupation, and place of residence. All our thoughts, actions, habit patterns, and experiences leave residues of karmic impressions that are stored as seeds in our personal memory bank. These latent seeds will germinate, sprout, and grow when stimulated by future conditions and experiences that resonate with the original imprints. They are the harbingers and embodiment of karma and will ripen as perfect justice.

The five aggregates may be seen in operation during a hypothetical sitting meditation practice. After watching my breath for a while, my sit-bone begins to ache. A thought demands a shift in position to alleviate my pain. So I move a little, make adjustments and resume observing my breathing, thoughts, feelings, and sounds. After a period of dynamic quietude, an image of an angel appears in front of me. It transforms into a brilliant golden light, which enters the crown of my head and settles in my heart center. An indescribable bliss permeates my being. Love radiates from my heart. My inner and outer worlds respond to the blessing.

The breath, sit-bone, chair, angel, light, crown, heart center, and world make up the aggregate of form. The pain and bliss comprise the aggregate of feeling. The recognition of the objects, physical and mental, is the aggregate of perception. The volition to move, the attachment to the image, the glory of the experience, and the intention to share the love make up the aggregate of mental formations. The awareness of breathing, pain, thought arising, body moving, quietness, image appearing, image transforming, bliss arising, and love radiating is the aggregate of consciousness.

This meditation practice took place completely in the realm of the aggregates. All of these aggregates were conditioned by the sense of being a separate self entity. Where in this description of a meditation process is there a *self*? Where in the list of the five aggregates is a *self* found? Starting with an examination of the form aggregate, when I look at you from the front, I recognize your face or your eyes. If I look at you from the back, I may still recognize you because of your hair style. But clearly, you are not your face, eyes, or hair. Those are merely the bases from which I identify you. On continuing the examination of you and I, the conclusion reached is that you are a bag of not-you(s) and I am a sack of not-I(s). So, is there a single, independent, and permanently existing entity present, or is *self* simply the name given to a set of aggregates as a whole?

The Self and Spaciousness

In the context of seeking reality, the renowned fourteenth century Buddhist philosopher Tsong-kha-pa summarizes a way of becoming free of bondage to the illusion of self:

> *The reality you seek to attain—the embodiment of truth—is total extinction of conceptions of both the self and that which belongs to the self. First, having contemplated in dismay the faults and disadvantages of cyclic existence, develop a wish to be done with it. Then research its roots, considering what might be the root cause of cyclic existence. You will thereby become certain from the depths of your heart that the reifying view of the perishing aggregates—or ignorance—acts as the root of cyclic existence.*

There are two approaches to destroying that root. The intellectual method tries to understand the analysis that refutes the normal conception of our self. The experiential approach is the meditation practice of shamatha and vipashyana that looks deeply into the nature of the *self*.

Based on logic and reasoning, the Buddha taught the view of emptiness or spaciousness (Skt., *shunyata)*. This analysis unerringly points out the fact that the self only exists dependently; it has no independent intrinsic existence—its existence is merely imputed. Self is the name we give to the body/mind complex with all of its endlessly changing parts. That which we call the self is precisely the collection of the five aggregates. By carefully looking at each of the aggregates, it is seen that none contains nor constitutes an inherent *self* because each one is constantly changing and is dependent on a variety of causes and conditions. According to Walpola Rahula's interpretation of the Buddha's words:

When the aggregates arise, decay and die, O monk,
Every moment you are born, decay and die.

Also, there is no inherent *self* outside of the aggregates because by definition and observation, the aggregates are all-inclusive. Since each of the aggregates has no inherent self-nature then the collective aggregates are said to be empty of self. Although appearance and function are evident, the self has no intrinsic self-nature. Again, self is simply a convenient label to apply to these aggregates operating together. Moreover, this fictional label is an illusory reification we use to propagate a form of collusion between my-self and your-self. Thus the existence of *you and I* as separate entities abiding in *egonorance* is dubiously verified to our mutual satisfaction. This agreement ensures the credible application of possessive pronouns. Dividing phenomena into me and mine, let the mischief begin!

The other approach to destroying the root of ignorance is through the union of shamatha and vipashyana—calm abiding and insight. Examination of selflessness enables the direct apprehension of the essence of no-self. Thereby, the root of confusion that clings to and reifies an illusory self is cut. We then recognize the ignorance that causes sorrow and inevitably traps us aboard the carousel of samsara and gives rise to the cycles of birth, life, death, and rebirth. This understanding consecrates the sacred union and allows us to dwell in the dynamic serenity that sees into the emptiness of self. Thus liberation from suffering is accomplished and the peace of nirvana is experienced.

Meditation Session Eleven

As your mind and body relax, be aware of thoughts and emotions arising. Search for and try to identify your self in this process. If a separate independent self cannot be found in this bag of blood and bones or body of light, then where is the entity that is searching?

No need to hurry to arrive at a conceptual conclusion; rather, you may notice a loosening of the attachment to the *searcher*. Rest in that awareness and leave things as they are.

Chapter Ten

Wheel of Dharma

In the "first turning of the wheel of dharma", the Buddha taught the pervasiveness of suffering and the way to end suffering. This first teaching cycle culminated with the concept of egoless-ness—the absence of a real self entity or personal self as discussed in Chapter Nine, "Origin of the Self". After a suitable period of gestation, the Buddha attended to a flock of relatively mature spiritual seekers at Vulture Peak Mountain near Rajagriha, India. There he gave the "second turning of the wheel of dharma". This assembly of disciples had committed themselves to a life of altruism and dharma practice and were therefore ripe for the next stage. This cycle of teachings further expounded the view of emptiness or shunyata, and included four core teachings referred to as the "Four Seals". These are not mystical revelations but stamps of authenticity—observable facts subject to verification by penetrating examination. These realities are summarized as:

1. All compounded things are impermanent.
2. All emotions and attachments are suffering, sooner or later.
3. All phenomena are illusory and have no inherent independent existence.
4. Nirvana is peace beyond concepts.

The First Reality

All things and phenomena are impermanent. The Buddha included the word "compounded" to emphasize the implication of the third seal that all things are merely assembled parts and do not exist independently Whether as a farmer watching the seasons change, a mother seeing her toddler grow, an adolescent experiencing mood swings, a scientist observing the uncertain behavior of subatomic particles, or an innocent resident becoming a hurricane victim, we are constantly reminded of the truth of the first seal—the fact of impermanence.

Even as we recognize this fact, Dzongsar Khyentse Rinpoche says that we are still ". . . caught up in compounding and fabricating reality with hopes of achieving long-lasting happiness. Wishing for 'happily ever after' is nothing more than a desire for permanence in disguise. We intend to establish ourselves and our world, but we forget that the corrosion begins as soon as creation begins. What we aim for is not decay, but what we do leads directly to decay." He points out that by being aware of assembled phenomena, we become aware of the interdependence of all things. Interdependence refers to the state of profound connectedness between all phenomena. Our very existence depends on the sun and this planet's hospitality. The food we eat comes from the efforts of others. The oxygen we breathe comes from trees and plants; in return, we give back our carbon dioxide. All our stuff: cell phones , movies, cars, clothing, etc. is provided by the skill and labor of others. Recognition of the role of interdependence in sustaining our happiness allows us to appreciate the truth of impermanence. He says, "Such awareness prevents us from getting caught up in all kinds of personal, political, and relationship dramas." Seeing the truth of this, we are less likely to be enslaved by our assumptions and hardened beliefs.

The Second Reality

This second reality was discussed in the Chapter Five subheading, "Four Noble Truths", under the topic of the *suffering of change*. There we found that in addition to the obviously painful emotions such as envy and anger, even the attachment of love could become suffering through jealousy or grief. All emotions are born from the root of the misunderstanding of our real identity and are midwifed by selfishness. The origin of our emotions is fundamentally flawed; yet we give credence to illusory feelings as if they really existed. Emotions arise when particular causes and conditions come together. For example, if someone criticizes me, my feelings are hurt. If someone flatters me, I feel exuberant. If someone steals my lover, I become enraged. Dzongsar Rinpoche says, "The moment we accept those emotions, the moment we buy into them, we have lost awareness and sanity. To eliminate suffering, you must generate awareness and tend to your emotions."

The Third Reality

The third reality is based on the Buddha's observation that all phenomena, all things known through the senses, are in the same sinking boat as the illusory self; they too have no intrinsic existence. Let us look into the question of the existence of things, of phenomena, with the same type of analysis used in Chapter Eight, "Search for the Self" where the reality of a separate self was refuted.

Does a car truly exist? We recognize that a car is comprised of a unique group of parts configured in a particular way so that they function as a car. It is a system made up of tires, brakes, motor, paint, windows, etc. But wherein is the car? Is the car in the parts or outside the parts? It cannot be in the parts for the parts themselves are comprised of more parts. Obviously, the car is not outside the parts. Perhaps the car is in the atoms forming it. If so, is it the top or bottom or one of the sides of an atom? And so the argument goes, ad infinitum.

Intellectually, we may understand that a car is just a label, a name, whose existence is merely imputed. Emotionally, however, if we have a shiny new car and it gets scratched, then what is the quality of our understanding of its non-existence?

In reality, the car has no inherent existence and is empty of an independent car -nature. Nevertheless, the fact that the car, like the self, appears and functions is undeniable; it is not a void—a nothingness. The higher truth holds that all phenomena lack intrinsic existence; everything is *shunyata or empti-ness.* Realization of the fact that the entire cosmos is merely an appearance gives us the freedom to avoid getting caught up in meaningless dramas. Knowing this, if our car gets scratched, we will not cry too much. We will no longer vest power in the illusion of duality. Our conflictual relationship with life will become transformed into a dance with samsara.

Although useful, intellectual analysis only yields a superficial understanding of reality. Because of our deeply established, ingrained thought habit patterns, the analytical approach alone will not liberate us from the bonds of delusion. The essential truth of shunyata or spaciousness is beyond conception and description and is only realized through right meditation.

The Fourth Reality

Nirvana literally means to extinguish or blow out. It is both the extinguishing of the fires that cause suffering and liberation from the prison of samsara. These fires are the poisons of attachment, aversion, and ignorance. When the fires are extinguished, pure consciousness remains untouched by the ashes of suffering. Dzongsar Rinpoche points out that the Buddha's path does not ultimately lead to a mere personal happiness. It is a road to freedom from suffering—from delusion and confusion for all sentient beings. He says "Thus nirvana is neither happiness nor unhappiness—it goes beyond such dualistic concepts. Nirvana is peace."

There is a peace that passes understanding; it abides in the hearts of those who have gone to the "other shore"—to those who dwell in timelessness. If nirvana is truly beyond concepts, then can one truly speak of it? Let us simply allow the question to gestate.

Dependent Origination

The Buddha taught that our existential situation arises from a continuously linked chain of causes:

From a beginning, ignorance is.
From ignorance of our real identity,
mistaken thoughts and habit patterns take shape.
From these mental formations,
rebirth-consciousness arises.
From this separate-self-consciousness,
we take name and form.
Sense organs arise and contact occurs.
Sensations manifest as attraction and repulsion.
Desire and craving precede grasping and clinging.
From this chain of causes and conditions,
we create our rebirth drama,
Thus, the cycle of birth, old age, and death repeats.
For this earthbound wanderer—a dancer in samsara
the cycle continues ad infinitum,
until realization dawns.

Samsara

Western philosophy (the way most people view the world) sees through the limited lens of dualism—the theory that everything can be reduced to two independent principles such as: God and the universe, good and evil, and body and mind. Classical science approaches reality through the dualistic belief that only matter and energy exist; although, modern quantum physics seems to be inclined towards a view of non-duality when confronting the interaction of consciousness and the measurement of reality. Neuroscientists view the brain as the mind and believe consciousness to be an epiphenomena of the brain's neurochemical activity. Psychologists and psychiatrists examine mental processes in patients and try to correct them through modifying their behavior or prescribing drugs to alter their brain chemistry. Nevertheless, neither group is concerned with the nature of consciousness or the mind.

The philosophical worldview of Buddhism is nondual in nature. This does not mean that all things are one, but that they are not-two. Nothing exists on its own because all phenomena are interdependent. On the surface, bipolar concepts such as *hot/cold*, *subject/object*, *thought/thinker*, *subject/object* appear to involve two different concepts, but they are really not separate–like two sides of a coin or two ends of a stick. There can be no *hot* without *cold* because what is hot to one is cold to another. There is no absolute hot or cold, each only has meaning in relation to the other. Ask a polar bear and a Sahara desert dweller to elaborate on this idea.

Our experience of the world has been conditioned by our dualistic state of mind that sees ourselves as separate individuals. This fundamental mistake creates the dualistic categories of self and other. Ultimately, the only absolute is the nondual union of mind and matter—pure consciousness, which apprehends reality.

Thinking of our self as a separate ego is the erroneous view that causes the operation of a recursive pattern of consciousness. This pattern identifies with and seeks to sustain the continuity of an illusory self-center. Where there is a self-center, selfishness arises and the concepts of me and mine are created. This false view leads to division and conflict and thus provides fertile soil for breeding attachment, aversion, greed, and anger. From these afflictions, perpetual suffering arises. Recognition of these facts attenuates the habit of selfishness and causes us to become kinder and gentler—softer around the edges like a ripened fruit. Realization occurs with the deconstruction of *the delusion of ego* and forms the basis for a transpersonal psychology of being and a way of living that alleviates the suffering of our self and others. Thus, *original sin* is not set in concrete, there is a way out of our existential predicament.

To profoundly see into this patterning is the fruit of the union of mindfulness and insight meditation. The revered twentieth century Tibetan Buddhist teacher and meditation master Tulku Urgyen Rinpoche pointed out in his book, *Vajra Speech*: "The extraordinary shamatha resting in the stillness free from conceptual thinking should be combined with the extraordinary vipashyana, which is recognizing the nature of that stillness." In that way, shamatha and vipashyana—mindfulness and insight are unified. This is the indivisibility of awareness and emptiness.

Meditation Session Twelve

As you relax into the silence, look into the nature of that serenity and calm abiding. Who is resting? Who is asking? After a few moments, stop seeking answers and let things be as they are.

Chapter Eleven

Recapitulation

We began this journey of inquiry from the certainty of thinking that we are a real separate self to the uncertainty of knowing precisely who we are. Our mode of being is dominated by a fictional character, the movie star, "I". Perhaps we have seen the shadows of the bars of our prison of delusion. During this journey, we exposed a precious jewel—the potential for radical transformation back into our original nature of primordial purity. However, as Chokyi Nyima Rinpoche points out: "Unless we can recognize and sustain the continuity of original wakefulness, deluded experience will not end." According to the Apocryphal Gospel of Thomas, Jesus said to his disciples: "Why ask about the end? For in the place in yourselves where you find the beginning, you will also find the end."

Our journey of awakening is a movement from the dark space of chaos, anxiety, and confusion to the bright space of clarity, joy, and luminosity. This path culminates in liberation and all-encompassing compassion. Liberation is the unfettered freedom from conditioning and suffering. Compassion is beyond sympathy and sorrow; it is a boundless radiant open-heartedness towards all beings.

Primordial Heritage

In the clarity of unveiled perception,
vast spaciousness and openness
comprise the universe and its inhabitants.

Timelessly—before a beginning,
Mind was pristine, unconditioned, and receptive.
Things appeared but no concepts formed.
Perceptions were direct and intuitive—
gracefully unnamed.
Mind abided in its own luminous clarity.

In our journey of return,
back to genesis,
The blessing of empowerment
enables the view of our primordial source.

The way of meditation resolves the mind
in its natural state—
innate compassion and lucidity.

Having ventured into the depths of samsara,
Having danced and twirled
in illusion's ballroom for countless ages,
The prodigal returns home
to receive its birthright,
the beatitude of awakening.

Continuing the Journey

On a plateau near the top of the mountain, meditation gardens nurture the seeds of enlightenment. Blossoms of kindness and compassion display evidence of their sprouting. The potential is there to be empowered to live a life of sanity and meaningfulness if we so choose. Our status on this path may be known through awareness of our actions, thoughts, feelings, and relationships. Unexpected opportunities for contact with qualified spiritual teachers may begin to arise.

Chokyi Nyima Rinpoche says: "The awakened state of a Buddha is one of perceiving clearly, distinctly and completely the nature of things and all that exists. It is a wisdom that knows things as they are without confusion, without distortion. This is why we ordinary human beings cannot avoid seeking support in the words and teachings of a Buddha."

With the intent to also liberate other sentient beings from suffering, we may continue the journey of awakening through joyful perseverance. Although the continuing path must be traveled alone, at this point it is crucial to find an authentic guide to support our aspirations. The right teacher will point out the appropriate way for each of us. We must carefully examine the teacher for qualities of kindness and compassion, detachment from worldly aims, utter selflessness, and a measure of realization. Charismatic speakers with a horde of groupie followers may not be a good choice. Ask yourself if there is the potential for a feeling of trust to develop between you and the teacher. To receive the blessings and empowerment of commitment, bring this search into your meditation practice.

The mystic poet and Indian saint Kabir makes lucid the subtleties of treading this path without wise advice (adapted from Robert Bly's translation):

Friend, please tell me what I can do about this world
I hold to, and keep spinning out!
I gave up sewn clothes, and wore a robe, but I noticed one
day the cloth was well woven.
So I bought some burlap, but I still throw it
elegantly over my left shoulder.
I pulled back my sexual longings, and now I discover
that I'm angry a lot.
I gave up rage, and now I notice that I am greedy
all day.
I worked hard at dissolving the greed, and now I am
proud of myself.
When the mind wants to break its link with the world
it still holds on to one thing.
Kabir says: Listen my friend, there are very few
that find the path!

To engage with the action that enables liberation, we must have the faith and confidence to embody the truths we encounter. In his *Flight of the Eagle*, Krishnamurti points out that one must lay the foundation of righteous behavior; otherwise, meditation is really a form of self-hypnosis. That foundation is built on the solid rock of the transcendental virtues previously discussed. Unless our daily life is free from afflictions, he says "the distortion of personal fear, anxiety, greed and so on, meditation has very little meaning."

In the *Voice of the Silence*, Helena the Theosophist records:

> *To reach Nirvana one must reach self-knowledge, and*
> *Self-knowledge is of loving deeds the child.*

The precious teacher of ninth century Tibet, Padmasambhava, the Lotus Born, was asked by the Lady Tsogyal: "How to practice the six paramitas?" He replied:

> *When you do not harbor any stinginess or prejudice whatsoever in your mind,*
> *That is the paramita of generosity.*
> *When you can skillfully relinquish your disturbing emotions,*
> *That is the paramita of discipline.*
> *When you are totally free from anger and resentment,*
> *That is the paramita of patience.*
> *When you are neither lazy nor indolent,*
> *That is the paramita of diligence.*
> *When you are free from distraction and attachment to the taste of meditation,*
> *That is the paramita of concentration.*
> *When you are utterly free from constructed concepts,*
> *That is the paramita of discriminating knowledge.*

Avoiding Extremes

After many years of asceticism, discipline, and self-mortification, a somewhat religious man, in conversation with Krishnamurti, spoke of the wonderful visions, powers, and experiences he had enjoyed as a result of his meditation practice; they filled him with satisfaction, gratification, self-confidence, and a proud sense of self-mastery. But, as he listened to himself, he began to question the meaning of the whole process. In his *Commentaries on Living*, Krishnamurti responded to his implicit query: "After all, what is essential is self-knowledge, which brings about a still mind. A still mind is not the product of will, of discipline, of the various practices to subjugate desire. All these practices and disciplines only strengthen the self, and virtue is then another rock on which the self can build a house of importance and respectability. The mind must be empty of the known for the unknowable to be. Without understanding the ways of the self, virtue begins to clothe itself in importance." On seeing the truth in this response, the man further asked how to get free of these self-constructed prison walls. Krishnamurti replied: "The very awareness that they must go is enough. Any action to break them down sets in motion the desire to achieve, to gain, and so brings into being the conflict of the opposites, the experiencer and the experience, the seeker and the sought. To see the false as the false is in itself enough, for that very perception frees the mind from the false."

Meditation sessions will be more productive if we lighten up our attitude and engage the meditation practice with joy. Let us not take our self too seriously. There once was a man who took a rather extreme approach to meditation practice. He deemed it necessary to sit with "knitted brow" upon a leopard skin in a full lotus position. So he sat for hours every day for three years enduring the misery of aching knees and joints until he became accustomed to the pain. After more years of sitting practice, he exhibited a superficial virtuousness spawned not from spontaneous goodness but from habit patterns set by extreme discipline. Manifesting a rigorously controlled mind, he became humorless and pious under the cover of disguised narcissism. His ill-conceived and degenerative meditation practice had yielded bitter fruit. Also, he could hardly walk.

Problem of Distraction

Preoccupation with avoiding distractions in connection with meditation practice gives life to obstacles. Bodily discomforts, external annoyances, and the internal mental disarray of thoughts and feelings readily become opportunities to experience attentiveness and detachment. When attention strays from the meditation object to intrusive thoughts, recognize the intruders and let them be. It's okay to allow them to loiter harmlessly in the fringes as attention returns to the meditation object. Distractions thus become friends. The point of mindfulness is to be aware of disturbing thoughts and responses to them. There is no need to chase after them or become attached to their content.

The registration of distracting conditions is the beginning of freedom from them and a fundamental sign of success in the meditation practice. As awareness deepens, experience the true nature of the mind in distraction—that thoughts are merely the spontaneous response or manifestation of *awareness* itself.

Session Protocol

All sense organs should be open during the meditation practice session; therefore, allow the eyes to remain open and without movement (except for natural blinking). Closing the eyes is a recursive habit carried over from previous customs and is unnecessary here. This openness is a symbolic and useful support to facilitate the continuity of the practice into daily life.

Connecting with the significance of the manner of opening and closing a practice session is important. The purpose of "setting the stage" at the start is to confirm our motivation to prepare an auspicious environment for the benevolent forces of nature to participate. "Sealing the practice" at the end with the expression of gratitude and generosity multiplies the effect of the practice. It preserves the ambience developed in the session and allows insight to flourish. Closing the session in this manner also shares the benefit with others.

The concept of time takes many forms in relation to meditation sessions: the clock times of beginning and ending, the duration of each session, the frequency of sessions, and our natural circadian rhythm. However, conceptual or psychological time, which is thought, has no relation to meditation itself. Nevertheless, time must be accommodated to schedule mundane obligations around the meditation practice session: but the clock need not be the master. Sages advise short sessions, many repetitions. End the session or take a break when the freshness or clarity of awareness begins to wane.

Post Meditation Sessions

What to do after the meditation practice session? If there is no continuity from the session to our mode of being in everyday life, then the practice sessions have been barren. While out walking, washing dishes, or commuting to work, pause for a moment and gather your faculties. Without changing posture or mood, without recalling the meditation practice protocols, simply open your sense gates and observe the present moment. This is the continuity of meditation. While lying in bed, just before sleep arrives, expand your awareness, outer and inner, and let everything be as it is.

The nature of the wheel of samsara is to spin in chronic confusion while we experience the afflictions of ignorance, greed, and malice. The demons of delusive thoughts and poisonous emotions are addressed through the practice of mindfulness meditation, which is to simply be aware of their arising, abiding, and dissolving. This meditation practice does not prevent thoughts and feelings from occurring but merely provides antidotes to counteract the poisons of those that display destructive power.

Not knowing the reality of how things are is the affliction of ignorance, stupidity, or dullness. The effects of delusion are numerous, wide ranging, and difficult to untangle but may be effectively dealt with through study, reflection, and insight meditation practice. Excessive desire is the overwhelming obsession to grasp and cling to attractive objects, whereas natural desire is a relatively passive longing to fulfill a need. The feeling of anger may range from a slight irritation or annoyance to a raging inferno. Fear ranges from a slight tingling in the solar plexus to gut wrenching panic or terror. Jealousy and envy also have their extremes.

Buddhists traditionally deal with poisonous emotions in three different ways according to their cultural background and the particular *turning of the wheel of dharma* that they are following. All begin by acknowledging the arising of the emotion and are motivated to mitigate its harmful effect by looking deeper into the actual nature of the feeling or emotion.

Theravada monks (Southern Buddhists) who focus on the *first turning*, which teaches the truth of suffering and the absence of a separate self nature, try to eliminate the poison. For example, if a feeling of lust towards an attractive person arises, this practitioner consciously imagines that person as a compounded phenomena made up of body parts: a sack of blood, bones, organs, and waste products. The object begins to appear less desirable when viewed in this manner. Practicing like this weakens that habit pattern.

Mahayana followers (Northern Buddhists) who focus on the *second turning*, which emphasizes compassion for all beings, wish to transform the poison. For example, if a malicious person deliberately inflicts pain on someone, this practitioner visualizes the bully tenderly holding and nurturing a precious baby or carefully rescuing a wounded bird. Thus, the initial feeling of anger will be transformed into loving kindness. Again, this practice will soften the sharp edges of the emotion.

Himalayan practitioners who focus on the *third turning*, which includes the first two with an emphasis on skillful means, take a more direct approach. For example, if anger arises, this practitioner looks directly at the feeling and knows it for what it is: their own mental offspring, a projection of their mind. For the beginner, the anger will definitely disappear - momentarily, but will come right back. However, continuing this practice will weaken the anger response until it becomes just another morning mist dissipated by the sunlight.

Let us look at a suggested strategy for approaching a full blown storm of anxiety.

1. Notice the anxiety or fear as it first arises in the mind. Is it an emotion of fear or dread? Is there a corresponding sensation in the body? Is a particular thought associated with it? Without analyzing its cause, simply focus on the feeling's presence. Carefully and precisely name it. Embrace it with care and compassion and allow an experience of clarity to unfold. Try to pinpoint its location within or outside the body. Allow the naked feeling to reveal itself so that its movement may be observed.

2. To fully recognize and identify the feeling, the masks of guilt, blame, or origin must be removed. Do not judge the feeling or place blame on anyone, but simply acknowledge the feeling.

3. After diligently searching, if the feeling cannot be found, then its last mask—its name is exposed and all associated thoughts and feelings dissolve together with the anxiety.

4. In the aftermath of the death of the anxiety, we may feel the presence of a nurturing energy—the fire of penetrating awareness and a sense of liberation.

Ultimately, there will be no line of demarcation between the formal meditation session and the post-meditation activity. Our mind and conduct freshened by the clarity and equanimity of the meditation practice allows us to skillfully dance with samsara.

Conclusion

This book's meditation practice schema of thirteen sessions is designed to encourage the practitioner to effortlessly relax into a profoundly subtle and interiorly oriented state. Progressing in nuanced stages, each session generates wholeness— coherent and peaceful. This approach establishes the foundation for the process of coming into relationship with the fruits of meditation—radiant love and luminous clarity. Gradually, the self—the subject, will fade into the background without trauma. The movement of meditation begins with looking at the contents of consciousness and continues with seeing the processes of thought until we apprehend the nature of mind. Meditation is complete when we lose ourselves in the purity of primordial awareness. The first practice, "Meditation Session One" is a most profound play of pure awareness. Since it is foundational and can be done anytime, anyplace, it is the go-to or default practice of choice.

Meditative experience comes through the openness and alert receptivity of our undistracted awareness. The union of shamatha and vipashyana gives rise to the samadhi of suchness or nonconceptual wakefulness. Realization of emptiness is the direct manifestation of the nature of mind in the form of compassion. Chokyi Nyima Rinpoche provides the following advice:

Don't veil your natural face within the grip of a

meditator and his object.
Now is the time for direct experience!
The sign of experience is your nature turning gentle.
Faith and devotion spring forth spontaneously.
Love and compassion naturally well up.
The ocean of understanding and experience overflows.

Song of Realization

In the year of the Water Dog (1742), the Seventh Dalai Lama composed a joyful song of meditative realization (Glenn Mullin's translation revisited):

An image of the sun enthroned in the heavens,
Radiating countless beams of light:
May one shower bright rays of love upon all living beings.
O, How excellent!

An image of a kingly eagle gliding high in space:
May one's mind soar without grasping in the space of truth itself, clear and void.
O, How excellent!

An image of fresh, white clouds, bright, pure and drifting freely:
May one perfect clarity and blissful absorption in the glorious mystic mandala.
O, How excellent!

An image of a mighty wind blowing gracefully through the sky:
May one sustain an energy flow beneficial to others, the best of spiritual practices, completely uncontrived.
O, How excellent!

An image of the vast sky everywhere free of obstruction:
May this song on emptiness, meditation, and action without hindrance benefit the world.
O, How excellent!

Meditation Session Thirteen

This concluding meditative practice takes place in the empty projection of a center-less, boundary-less sphere. Bring to mind a luminous apparition of a sphere and enter into it. Therein are no directions. You will not move to the center for there is no you and no center. Let the periphery fade into the infinite for there are no limits in meditation.

Descriptive terms such as vast, ineffable, openness, blissful, or boundlessly compassionate are completely inadequate to convey the experience of meditation. Nevertheless, the nectar of meditation may flavor all worldly actions and relationships with nonattachment, compassion, clarity, and love. Open your awareness into that immense, thunderous, pregnant silence of spaciousness. Rest alertly in the non-meditation of pure be-ness—nonconceptual naked awareness!

Epilogue

In order to see the world as it is, Ludwig Wittgenstein's final advice for transcending his own philosophical propositions informs the entirety of Chapter Seven of his *Tractatus* with the apologetic:

What we cannot speak about,
We must pass over in silence.

Matters too subtle for discourse—such as emptiness are best approached vis-à-vis immersion in the pristine meditation of luminous wakefulness. That which we have understood, we may hold with care and tentativeness. That which we have seen as false, simply let go. That which we have not yet understood, let gestate in calm abiding. Lastly, know that the outer signs of success in meditation practice are the display of a little more kindness and a little less selfishness. The inner signs are the welling up of love, compassion, and boundless empathy and equanimity. All other signs are suspect.

Immense gratitude is expressed for the essential guidance of the Buddha and other lucent ones, pioneers who have traveled this path and left signposts. Gleaning from their pure harvest, hopefully, nothing of my own has contaminated their teaching. I acknowledge the substance of this pretentious treatise: the ideas, the concepts, the viewpoints, and the style were uninhibitedly drawn from many named and unnamed sources. In the end, there is no method for attaining enlightenment, yet in the beginning there must be effort, without which the end cannot be approached. The purpose of this journey along the paths of meditation is to bridge the gap between our current status as existentially delusional beings and the other shore of liberation. It is up to the sojourner to cross over. May all beings be happy and free from suffering. May joy and peace abide within every heart and mind.

Glossary

bodhicitta (Sanskrit.) - Awakened mind of compassion; the aspiration to attain enlightenment in order to benefit all sentient beings.

bodhisattva (Skt.) - Someone who has developed bodhicitta—the pure wish to help others.

dharma (Skt.) - The Buddha's teachings. Depending on the context, "dharma" can mean phenomena or mental objects, as well as attributes or qualities. Prior to the Buddha's time, it usually meant duty or law.

esoteric – Refers to the inner or core concepts of various religious denominations that are held to be their deeper truths. Buddhism has its Vajrayana or tantric tradition; Islam has its Sufi tradition; Christianity relates to the Gnostic and Jewish Essene traditions; Judaism has the Kabbalist and Hasidic traditions. There are also other philosophical esoteric traditions such as the Esoteric School of Theosophy, the Pythagorean School, Co-masonry, and Neoplatonism.

Five Aggregates - Form, feeling, perception, mental formations, and consciousness

Four Immeasurables - Loving-kindness, compassion, joy, and equanimity

Four Noble Truths - 1) the truth of suffering: all delusion-driven life is suffering; 2) the truth of origin: the cause of that suffering is misunderstanding reality; 3) the truth of cessation: there is a way out of suffering; and 4) the truth of the path: a right way of living based on spiritual education in morality, meditation, and wisdom.

Four Realities - core Buddhist teachings often referred to as the "Four Seals". These are ordinary facts subject to verification by penetrating examination. Summarized as: 1) all compounded things are impermanent; 2) all emotions and attachments are painful; 3) all phenomena are illusory with no real existence; and 4) nirvana is peace beyond concepts.

Four Reminders (Aka Four Mind Changings by Buddhist practitioners) - Observable facts regarding everyone's present status of being. They include the preciousness of this human life, impermanence and death, the action of karma, and the defects of samsara.

karma (Skt.) - The universal law of cause and effect. It is not preordained fate: as the Bible says *whatsoever a man soweth, that shall he also reap*. The actions of karma are extremely subtle and complex because the relationship between cause and effect depends on a multitude of unknown conditions—primarily the motivation of the doer.

meditation - Seeing one's intrinsic nature—how things really are

paramita (Skt.) - Refers to having crossed the "river of suffering" to the "other shore of peace and awakening." The six paramitas are generosity, discipline, patience, enthusiasm, mindfulness, and wisdom.

reincarnation - A Buddhist doctrine that all sentient beings die and are reborn in new bodies life after life until they liberate themselves from ignorance and attain enlightenment. The theory of reincarnation linked with the concept of karma forms a beautiful synthesis for understanding why bad things happen to good people. Causes set in motion by us in this or a previous life will surely play out.

samadhi (Skt.) - A state of undistracted concentration or meditative absorption. In some contexts it means stability in the awakened state

samsara (Skt.) - Our ordinary reality, an endless cycle of frustration and suffering generated as the result of karma. It refers to a vicious circle of birth and death and rebirth, characterized by suffering, impermanence, and ignorance. The state of ordinary sentient beings fettered by ignorance and dualistic perception, karma, and disturbing emotions.

Seal the Practice - Close each meditation practice session with an expression of generosity and gratitude. Project the wish that others may also benefit from your practice.

Set the Stage - Initiate the meditation practice session by providing the most favorable conditions in order to feel relaxed and at ease with no induced tensions in your mind or body.

Shakyamuni - honorific of the historical Buddha; sage of the Shakya clan

shamatha - Serenity meditation practice concerned with mindfulness and calming the mind in order to rest free from the disturbance of thoughts and feelings

Siddhartha Gautama - personal and family name of the prince who became the Buddha

shunyata (Skt.) - the union of cognizance and emptiness

theosophy - From the Greek, *theosophia,* or *divine wisdom.* It is an integration of religion, science, philosophy, and esotericism based on the *ageless wisdom* traditions. Truths revealed in these traditions are said to originally spring from the roots of spirit and form the core of all religions. Theosophy is not a religion but a referent to *religion* itself.

vipashyana (Skt.) - insight meditation practice concerned with gaining insight into the ultimate non-dual nature of reality. The Himalayan Buddhist tradition includes and goes beyond the Buddha's initial teachings on mindfulness.

vipassana (Pali) - the Buddha's initial teachings on mindfulness. Also known as insight meditation practice by popular Western meditation teachers, they emphasize mindfulness techniques involving the body and feelings in their vipassana meditation practice.

wu wei (Taoism) - the effortless spontaneous alignment with right action.

yoga (Skt.) - union or to yoke. In this context, yoga is that action necessary to unite consciousness with spirit, to marry pure awareness with the primordial natural condition of existence.

Credits and Consults

Annie Besant, *The Path of Discipleship* (Adyar, India: Theosophical Publishing House, 1980, c1910). Excerpt reprinted with permission from the publisher. www.adyarbooks.com

Bhagavad-Gita (Discourse VI, v. 18, 19).

H. P. Blavatsky, *Voice of the Silence*, verse 198 (Adyar, India: Theosophical Publishing House, 1968). Excerpt reprinted with permission from the publisher. www.adyarbooks.com

H. P. Blavatsky, *The Secret Doctrine,* vol. 1. Ed. Boris de Zirkoff (Wheaton, IL: Theosophical Publishing House, 1993). Excerpt reprinted with permission from the publisher. www.adyarbooks.com

Robert Bly, *The Kabir Book* (Boston: The Seventies Press, Beacon Press, 1977).

Mabel Collins, *Light on the Path* (Adyar: Theosophical Publishing House, 1968). Excerpt reprinted with permission from the publisher. www.adyarbooks.com

Thich Nhat Hanh, Transformation and Healing: Sutra on the Four Establishments of Mindfulness (Berkeley, CA: Parallax Press, 1990).

Chip Hartranft, *The Yoga-Sutra of Patanjali* (Boston: Shambhala Publications, 2003).

Hermann Hesse, *Steppenwolf* (Holt, Rinehart and Winston, Inc., 1929).

Ianthe Hoskins, ed., *Foundations of Esoteric Philosophy* (Adyar, India: Theosophical Publishing House, 2004). Excerpt reprinted with permission from the publisher. www.adyarbooks.com

Fr. Thomas Keating, *The Classical Practice of Lectio Divina* (http://www.contemplativeoutreach.org, 2008).

Dzongsar Jamyang Khyentse, *What Makes You Not a Buddhist* (Boston: Shambhala Publications, 2008).

Jiddu Krishnamurti, *Commentaries on Living, Second Series* (New York: Harper & Brothers, 1958). Excerpt reprinted with permission from Krishnamurti Foundation of America. www.kfa.org

Jiddu Krishnamurti, *The Flight of the Eagle* (New York: Harper & Row, 1971). Excerpt reprinted with permission from Krishnamurti Foundation of America. www.kfa.org

Jiddu Krishnamurti, *Freedom from the Known* (New York: Harper & Row, 1969). Excerpt reprinted with permission from Krishnamurti Foundation of America. www.kfa.org

Jiddu Krishnamurti, *Krishnamurti's Journal* (San Francisco: Harper & Row, 1982). Excerpt reprinted with permission from Krishnamurti Foundation of America. www.kfa.org

Jiddu Krishnamurti, *Krishnamurti's Notebook* (New York: Harper & Row, 1976). Excerpt reprinted with permission from Krishnamurti Foundation of America. www.kfa.org

Jiddu Krishnamurti, *Krishnamurti on Education* (India: Krishnamurti Foundation India, 1974). Excerpt reprinted with permission from Krishnamurti Foundation of America. www.kfa.org

Jiddu Krishnamurti, *Krishnamurti to Himself* (San Francisco: Harper & Row, 1987). Excerpt reprinted with permission from Krishnamurti Foundation of America. www.kfa.org

Dalai Lama, *The Way to Freedom* (India: Harper Collins, 1995).

Dalai Lama, *Dzogchen, The Heart Essence of the Great Perfection* (Ithaca, NY: Snow Lion Publications, 2000). Excerpt reprinted with permission from the publisher. www.snowlionpub.com

Brother Lawrence, *The Practice of the Presence of God* (Fleming H. Revell Company, MCMLVIII).

Rohit Mehta, *Yoga, The Art of Integration* (Adyar: Theosophical Publishing House, 1975). Excerpt reprinted with permission from the publisher. www.adyarbooks.com

Thomas Merton, *New Seeds of Contemplation* (New York: New Directions Publishing Corporation, 1961).

Glenn Mullin, *Meditations to Transform the Mind* (Ithaca, NY: Snow Lion Publications, 1999). Excerpt reprinted with permission from the publisher. www.snowlionpub.com

Padmasambhava, *Dakini Teaching* (Hong Kong: Rangjung Yeshe Publications, 1999). Excerpt reprinted with permission from the publisher.

Walpola Rahula, *What the Buddha Taught* (New York: Grove Press, 1974).

Chokyi Nyima Rinpoche, *The Bardo Guidebook* (Hong Kong: Rangjung Yeshe Publications, 1991).

Chokyi Nyima Rinpoche, *The Union of Mahamudra and Dzogchen* (Hong Kong: Rangjung Yeshe Publications, 1986). Excerpt reprinted with permission from the publisher.

Tsoknyi Rinpoche, *Fearless Simplicity* (Hong Kong: Rangjung Yeshe Publications, 2003).

Tulku Urgyen Rinpoche, *Vajra Speech* (Hong Kong: Rangjung Yeshe Publications, 2001). Excerpt reprinted with permission from the publisher.

Yongey Mingyur Rinpoche, *Turning Confusion into Clarity* (Boston and London: Snow Lion, 2014).

Idries Shaw, *The Way of the Sufi* (London: Octagon Press, 2004).

St. John of the Cross, *Dark Night of the Soul* (New York: Riverhead Books, 2002).

St. Teresa of Avila, *The Interior Castle* (New York: Riverhead Books, 2003).

I. K. Taimni, *Self-Realization through Love* (Adyar: Theosophical Publishing House, 1975). Excerpt reprinted with permission from the publisher. www.adyarbooks.com

Tsong-kha-pa, *The Great Treatise on the Stages of the Path to Enlightenment,* vol. 3 (Ithaca, New York: Snow Lion Publications, 2002). Excerpt reprinted with permission from the publisher. www.snowlionpub.com

Ken Wilber, The Eye of Spirit, An Integral Vision for a World Gone Slightly Mad (Boston: Shambhala Publications, Inc., 1997).

Ludwig Wittgenstein, *Tractatus Logico-Philosophicus* (London and New York: Routledge Classics, 2001).

About the Author

Cecil Messer, an ardent inquirer into the core values of spirituality, has practiced meditation under the guidance of qualified Tibetan Buddhist teachers since the beginning of this millennium. He presented classes at the Krotona School of Theosophy, Ojai, CA on meditation and spiritual teachings extracted from a variety of religious traditions and conducted a yearlong online seminar *Exploring the Heart of Meditation*. He has published related articles in national and international periodicals. Born in rural Alabama, he is a retiree of the NASA Space Program Science and Engineering Team. He currently resides in the mountains of North Carolina where he purports to be a dharma practitioner.

Made in the USA
Middletown, DE
02 December 2022

16490466R00137